The Partisan Sort

Chicago Studies in American Politics

A series edited by Benjamin I. Page, Susan Herbst, Lawrence R. Jacobs, and James Druckman

Also in the series:

The Partisan Sort

*How Liberals Became Democrats and
Conservatives Became Republicans*

MATTHEW LEVENDUSKY

THE UNIVERSITY OF CHICAGO PRESS   CHICAGO AND LONDON

MATTHEW LEVENDUSKY is assistant professor of political science at the University of Pennsylvania.

The University of Chicago Press, Chicago 60637
The University of Chicago Press, Ltd., London
© 2009 by The University of Chicago
All rights reserved. Published 2009
Printed in the United States of America
18 17 16 15 14 13 12 11 10 09   1 2 3 4 5

ISBN-13: 978-0-226-47364-2 (cloth)
ISBN-13: 978-0-226-47365-9 (paper)
ISBN-10: 0-226-47364-3 (cloth)
ISBN-10: 0-226-47365-1 (paper)

Library of Congress Cataloging-in-Publication Data

Levendusky, Matthew.
    The partisan sort : how liberals became Democrats and conservatives became Republicans / Matthew Levendusky.
        p.   cm.
    Includes bibliographical references and index.
    ISBN-13: 978-0-226-47364-2 (cloth : alk. paper)
    ISBN-13: 978-0-226-47365-9 (pbk. : alk. paper)
    ISBN-10: 0-226-47364-3 (cloth : alk. paper)
    ISBN-10: 0-226-47365-1 (pbk. : alk. paper)
      1. Political parties—United States. 2. Voting research—United States. 3. United States—Politics and government—2001–   I. Title.
    JK2265.L39 2010
    324.273—dc22

                                                            2009016605

TO TOM, ROSE, KAY, TOM, AND DEB, FOR THEIR LOVE AND SUPPORT

Contents

Figures

Tables

Acknowledgments

Writing a book is no easy task, and in the process, I have accumulated debts to scholars and institutions far and wide. I am particularly grateful to the institutions that supported me while I wrote the bulk of this book: the Institution for Social and Policy Studies (and its director, Don Green), the Center for the Study of American Politics (and its director, Alan Gerber), and the Department of Political Science at the University of Pennsylvania. I also thank the Department of Political Science at Stanford University, where this project first took shape several years ago. My final institutional debt is to the Institute for the Study of Citizens and Politics at the Annenberg Public Policy Center (and its director, Diana Mutz), which generously funded the experiments described in chapter 5. Without the financial support of all these institutions, this book would simply not have been possible. I thank them all.

I have also accumulated debts to a large number of scholars, too many to list in this short space. In particular, I wish to extend my thanks to those scholars who generously read and commented on manuscript chapters: Scott Adler, Steve Ansolabehere, Julia Azaria, Daniel Bergan, Jake Bowers, David Brady, Morris Fiorina, Justin Fox, Alan Gerber, Donald Green, Jeff Green, Hahrie Han, Meghan Holohan, Greg Huber, Simon Jackman, Jon Krosnick, John Lapinski, Julia Lynch, David Mayhew, Diana Mutz, Jeremy Pope, Rogers Smith, and Paul Sniderman. Jacob Hacker deserves special recognition for reading a complete draft of the manuscript and providing especially timely commentary. If I have omitted anyone from this list, let me assure you that it is the quality of my memory—not the quality of your comments—that leads to your exclusion.

I owe a deep debt of gratitude to Jamie Druckman for helping me find a home at the University of Chicago Press; a similar debt extends to John

Tryneski and Rodney Powell for helping me navigate the mysteries of the publication process. I also thank the referees for their helpful and extensive comments on the manuscript; their insights improved the final product tremendously.

I close with thanks to two groups of individuals who have impacted not only this manuscript (albeit indirectly) but my whole career as a political scientist. Many years ago, when I was a wide-eyed undergraduate at Penn State, Bill Bianco and Frank Baumgartner convinced me that there was a future to studying political science and pushed me toward graduate school rather than law school. I leave it to the reader to decide if they deserve credit or blame for that decision.

Last but not least, my oldest and deepest debt is to Tom, Rose, Kay, Tom, and Deb. For as long as I can remember, they've always supported, encouraged, and grounded me. For that, I will always be grateful. I am proud to dedicate this book to them.

CHAPTER ONE

The Transformation of
the American Electorate

An observer studying the American electorate in the 1970s might well have concluded that party was on the wane. Both parties were ideologically heterogeneous, with sizable contingents of both liberals and conservatives at the mass and elite levels. Levels of split-ticket voting were relatively high, and party-line voting was lower than it had been in earlier decades. Noting these shifts, scholars—and popular commentators—argued that party no longer had much relevance to ordinary Americans.

Looking at the contemporary electorate, however, one reaches a fundamentally different conclusion. Party and ideology today are much more tightly aligned than they were a generation ago, with liberals and conservatives better sorted into the Democratic and Republican parties (though whether or not this has generated electoral polarization is less clear, as I explain below). Levels of party voting have surged to near-record levels, and split-ticket voting continues to decline. While some of the 2008 post-election commentary portrayed President Obama's win as ushering in a new "postpartisan" era, the exit poll data reveal that approximately 90 percent of Democrats and Republicans voted for their party's candidate, levels quite similar to those of other recent elections. Party has experienced a renaissance in American politics: far from being irrelevant to contemporary politics, party is once again the driving factor behind political behavior.

What explains this massive shift in the American electorate? Why are voters' partisan and ideological commitments so much more tightly

connected today than they were in previous decades? Why has party voting surged? I argue that the increasing polarization of political elites is a
primary factor driving these changes. In the 1950s and 1960s, Democratic
and Republican elites were relatively heterogeneous, with a liberal "Rocke-
feller Republican" wing and a cadre of conservative southern Democrats.
But by the 1990s and 2000s, elites were more sharply polarized, with most
Democrats on the left and most Republicans on the right. This elite-level
shift helps voters understand the set of policy positions that accompany
being a Democrat or a Republican. Voters then utilize these increasingly
clear cues to align their partisan and ideological beliefs. This tighter party-
ideology link in turn fuels the rise in party voting and has broad implications for how candidates run for office and relate to voters more generally.
So elite polarization, by clarifying what it means to be a Democrat or a
Republican, changes the organization of voters' preferences, which in turn
changes their behavior. This book tells the story of this shift in voters' attitudes and behavior.[1]

From Elites to Voters

There is broad agreement that partisan political elites have become more
divided since the late 1960s. Elite Democrats are now almost all liberals,
and elite Republicans are almost all conservatives, with very little ideological overlap between the parties (see, among others, Thierault 2008;
Sinclair 2006; McCarty, Poole, and Rosenthal 2006).[2] What is less clear is
how this increased elite polarization has impacted the mass public and,
in particular, whether or not this elite polarization has generated mass
polarization. Some scholars argue that it has—as elites have moved to the
ideological poles, ordinary voters have followed them. Voters today are
less centrist, and more ideologically extreme, than they were a generation ago. The electorate has "hollowed out" and is increasingly bimodal,
with only a small number of moderates remaining in the ideological
center (Abramowitz and Saunders 2008; Abramowitz 2006; Campbell
2006b).

But others challenge this claim, arguing that most voters are moderate
and centrist. These authors agree that elite polarization has increased,
but they disagree that this has led to the public becoming more polarized.
Instead, they argue that ordinary voters are no more polarized than they
were a generation ago, and Democratic and Republican voters still take

similar positions on many issues (e.g., Fiorina, Abrams, and Pope 2005; McCarty, Poole, and Rosenthal 2006; DiMaggio, Evans, and Bryson 1996; Baker 2005).

I take a moderate position between these two competing arguments. I argue that elite polarization has fundamentally transformed voters, but not by greatly increasing mass polarization. Instead, elite polarization has caused voters to adopt the ideological outlook of their same-party elites. I refer to this alignment of partisanship and ideology as *sorting;* sorted Democrats are liberals, and sorted Republicans are conservatives.[3]

This sorting is elite driven. As elites pull apart to the ideological poles, they clarify what it means to be a Democrat or a Republican. Ordinary voters use these clearer cues to align their own partisanship and ideology. Elite polarization, by clarifying where the parties stand on the issues of the day, causes ordinary voters to sort. This voter sorting come both from conversion (existing voters aligning their partisanship and ideology with one another) and from replacement (newer voters being more likely to enter the electorate already sorted). Further, I demonstrate that this sorting is not simply the product of changes in one region or group (e.g., the white South) or any one issue. Rather, sorting is a widespread, national phenomenon.

When an individual voter transitions from unsorted to sorted, he can make this adjustment in one of two ways. He can move his partisanship into alignment with his ideology (e.g., a liberal Republican becomes a liberal Democrat), or he can adjust his ideology to fit with his partisanship (e.g., a liberal Republican becomes a conservative Republican). I find that voters typically shift their ideology to fit with their party identification; ideology-driven party exit (changing one's party to fit with one's ideology) occurs in only a narrow set of circumstances.

This sorting has important implications for voter behavior and, in turn, candidate behavior as well. When a voter moves from unsorted to sorted, he becomes much more firmly anchored to his party and much more supportive of it both in the voting booth and beyond. As a result, sorting helps to explain recent electoral trends such as the growth of party voting, the decline of split-ticket voting, and the growth in attitudinal consistency observed over time. These electoral changes also have implications for elites. Campaigns can now devote more attention to their core supporters—their "base"—as a result of these sorting-driven changes in the electorate. Simply put, sorting is a major change in the American electoral landscape.

Defining Key Concepts

I argued above that sorting is an elite-driven process. But who are the "elites"? Throughout the book, whenever I refer to elites, I really am referring to "partisan political elites"—politicians holding elected office who have some control over policy (Zaller 1992; Lee 2002). Elites are members of Congress, presidential nominees, governors, and so forth—what Fiorina, Abrams, and Pope (2005) call the "political class."

Similarly, I argued that sorting is the alignment of partisanship and ideology without explicitly defining either term. My definition of "partisanship" comes from *The American Voter:* partisanship is an "individual's affective orientation toward an important group object in his environment" (Campbell et al. 1980, 121). This psychological attachment is crucial for ordinary voters because it forms the basis of their political identity and gives them a lens through which to view the political world. It is no exaggeration to argue that partisanship, more than almost any other variable, determines how voters see the political world (Bartels 2002).

Defining "ideology" is a bit more complicated. Ideology is a complex cluster of ideas encompassing not just a set of issue positions but also the connections between the issues themselves (e.g., how is one's position on abortion related to one's position on tax cuts?) and the connections between the issues and abstract concepts like liberalism and conservatism (Converse 1964; Gerring 1997). I set aside the complex question of assessing the connections between respondents' political attitudes and these abstract principles and underlying values. Instead, I focus here on *indicators* of ideology—respondents' liberal-conservative self-identification and their issue positions on a variety of different policies. While there is some controversy about the self-identification measure in the literature (Conover and Feldman 1981), I use it here as a summary indicator of the respondent's outlook on politics (for similar uses, see Zaller 1992; Hetherington 2001; Sniderman and Carmines 1997). Using both measures together will allow me to demonstrate that sorting is not simply an artifact of a particular measure.

Distinguishing Sorting from Polarization

Although I discussed sorting and polarization above, I did not clarify precisely how they are distinct from one another. Sorting is a changing correlation between partisanship and ideology, so that, in a sorted electorate, party and ideology are more closely related (more correlated) than in an

TABLE I.I **The difference between sorting and polarization**

Ideology	Time 1	Time 2
Example of Sorting:		
Democrats	50 liberals, 50 conservatives	80 liberals, 20 conservatives
Independents	100 moderates	100 moderates
Republicans	50 liberals, 50 conservatives	20 liberals, 80 conservatives
Overall electorate	100 liberals, 100 moderates, 100 conservatives	100 liberals, 100 moderates, 100 conservatives
Example of Mass Polarization:		
Democrats	50 liberals, 50 conservatives	100 liberals
Independents	100 moderates	50 liberals, 50 conservatives
Republicans	50 liberals, 50 conservatives	100 conservatives
Overall electorate	100 liberals, 100 moderates, 100 conservatives	150 liberals, 150 conservatives

unsorted electorate. Polarization, on the other hand, means that voters are adopting more ideologically extreme positions (e.g., a changing marginal distribution of ideology).[4] In a polarized electorate, attitudes are no longer primarily centrist and unimodal but rather have pushed toward the ideological extremes and are more bimodal—there are more voters at the extremes than in the center. In the limit, as polarization increases, the moderate voters—the centrists—will disappear altogether (see also Fiorina and Levendusky 2006b).[5]

The hypothetical electorate depicted in table 1.1 should help to clarify the difference between sorting and mass polarization. The upper half of the table depicts voter sorting. At time 1, both parties are barely distinguishable ideologically: Democrats and Republicans have similar numbers of liberals and conservatives, so knowing a voter's party identification gives very little information about his ideology. But between time 1 and time 2, the parties sort. At time 2, partisanship is much more tightly linked to ideology—most liberals are Democrats; most conservatives are Republicans. Knowing someone's ideology now makes it much more likely that one can correctly identify his partisanship.

Despite this sorting, the aggregate distribution of ideology remains the same at both time 1 and time 2—there are 100 liberals, 100 moderates, and 100 conservatives at both points in time. There are no more citizens on the extremes at time 2 than at time 1, and there is no evidence of bimodality at either point in time: the distribution of ideology is constant and uniform. This example, though contrived, makes it clear that sorting is a distinct phenomenon from mass polarization.

Some readers might prefer to use the term "partisan polarization" in lieu of "sorting": after all, as a result of sorting, the mass parties are more polarized (e.g., the Democrats are more uniformly liberal postsorting than they were presorting). I prefer to avoid the term "partisan polarization" on the grounds of clarity. Sorting and polarization are distinct phenomena and giving them different names reinforces this fact (see also Fiorina and Levendusky 2006b).[6]

The bottom half of table 1.1, by contrast, depicts a polarized electorate. Between time 1 and time 2, the electorate pulls apart to the ideological poles. All voters become either liberals or conservatives by time 2, which has two implications. It means, first, that there is no longer any overlap between the parties and second, that there is no one remaining in the center of the ideological distribution—the marginal distribution of ideology has changed. There has been movement away from the center and toward the extremes, and the distribution of ideology is now fully bimodal—opinion is quite literally polarized between liberals and conservatives.[7]

One could object to my sorting versus polarization distinction on the grounds that sorting will inevitably generate polarization (Abramowitz 2006). As voters adopt their party's positions, they move away from the center and toward the poles. For example, if a respondent goes from (say) being a moderate Democrat to a liberal Democrat, then he has moved away from the center and toward the liberal end of the spectrum. Aggregated over many respondents, this sorting will yield an increasingly polarized electorate. While this is certainly true, I will demonstrate later that this effect is fairly modest in scope. Even after sorting, most Americans remain at least as close to the ideological center as they do to the ideological poles, so the aggregate increase in mass polarization due to voter sorting is quite limited. When voters sort, they move from (say) moderate to slightly liberal but fall short of becoming very liberal. They may choose a side, but they do not move to the extremes. So while sorting does lead to somewhat greater polarization, it is erroneous to assume that a better-sorted electorate will inevitably become a deeply polarized electorate.

In effect, the distinction between polarization and sorting is a difference of degree rather than of kind. In both cases, voters are moving toward their political party's position. The difference is that, in an electorate that is simply better sorted, many voters will adopt their party's position without embracing the extreme version of it. In a polarized electorate, by contrast, not only have people chosen a side, but they have moved to the extremes (see table 1.1). This distinction is worth making on the grounds of clarity alone: we should know whether people are simply choosing a side, or whether they are embracing an extreme version of that side. Further, there is a practical difference as well: in a sorted electorate, a middle remains to negotiate conflicts between the two sides, which should facilitate compromise (Fiorina and Levendusky 2006a; Binder 1999). Sorting and polarization are different processes with different consequences and should be treated as distinct concepts.

Studying Voter Sorting

This study of sorting is an investigation of how voters align their party identification and ideological beliefs over time. But where do partisanship and ideology originate? Nearly all of the previous research on this question begins with a common assumption: mass opinions reflect the considerations present in elite opinions.[8] Ordinary voters typically do not devote the time and energy needed to become informed on even the most salient issues of the day (Berelson, Lazarsfeld, and McPhee 1954; Campbell et al. 1980; Converse 1964; Key 1966). How can voters overcome this lack of knowledge? They do so by turning to elites. Ordinary voters look to elites who share their partisan and ideological outlook and adopt those elites' positions as their own (Zaller 1992; Brody 1991; but see Lee 2002 for an alternative, bottom-up perspective).

Cue taking also provides a mechanism for explaining mass opinion *change*. Elites are constantly searching for new issue positions that will translate into a political advantage. But as they shift their positions, they also change the cue they send to ordinary voters about where the parties stand on the issue. As voters follow these new cues, the distribution of opinion in the mass electorate changes to reflect the new elite alignment. Mass-level opinion change stems from elite-level change (Sniderman and Levendusky 2007; Carmines and Stimson 1989; Stimson 2004).

Many scholars have used this elite-driven approach to study the general process of attitude change over time (see, among others, Carmines and Stimson 1989; Adams 1997; Layman 2001). In particular, a number of scholars have used it to explore how ordinary voters have responded to increasing levels of elite polarization. Elite polarization has generated a resurgence of mass partisanship, reversing the decline of mass partisanship noted in the 1970s and 1980s (Hetherington 2001; on the decline of parties, see Wattenberg 1998). This resurgence has been so robust that various indicators of partisanship are now as vigorous as they were during the 1950s, the previous apex of party in twentieth-century American politics (Bartels 2000). Not only is party identification now stronger than it was thirty years ago, it also may be more strongly related to issue positions and other ideological beliefs as a result of elite-level changes (see, among others, Fiorina and Levendusky 2006b; Abramowitz and Saunders 1998; Layman and Carsey 2002a).

The Missing Links in the Sorting Argument

Scholars have made important strides in articulating a theory of sorting in recent years, demonstrating that mass sorting exists and is linked to changes at the elite level. Despite this progress, however, at least two elements of a comprehensive account of sorting are missing from existing scholarship. First, all of the evidence to date connecting elite opinion to mass sorting comes from observational data. Elite polarization is clearly associated with mass sorting, but we lack any evidence that one actually causes the other. Scholars must move beyond recognizing that elite polarization and sorting are related to an understanding of how changes in elite polarization generate mass sorting. To make such claims possible, I incorporate original experimental evidence as well as large-scale national surveys into my argument in later chapters, thereby moving from correlation to causation.

Second, very little is known about the implications of sorting for voters themselves. Suppose a liberal Republican voter, after hearing the rhetoric of contemporary Republican elites, becomes a conservative. Does this shift from liberal Republican to conservative Republican affect his voting behavior? His affect toward the parties? His other political behaviors? The extant literature provides no satisfactory answers to these questions.

I fill this gap in the literature by demonstrating the sizable and surprising effects of sorting on voters' attitudes and behaviors. When a voter moves from unsorted to sorted, he becomes much more strongly attached to his party and becomes much more loyal to it in a variety of different ways. The growth in voter sorting, therefore, provides a causal mechanism that can account for part of the increase in party voting and the decline of split-ticket voting (Hetherington 2001; Bartels 2000), the growth of polarized evaluations (Shapiro and Bloch-Elkon 2006; Jacobson 2006), and the growth of attitude consistency in the mass public (Layman and Carsey 2002a). Sorting fundamentally changes how voters behave.

These individual-level changes have significant ramifications for *elite* behavior as well. For fifty years, political scientists—and political pundits—argued that campaigns should focus on identifying and converting undecided voters: the "swing" voters. Campaigns could essentially ignore their base—their most ardent, committed supporters—because these individuals would support their candidate regardless of what the campaign did (Downs 1957; Mayer 2008). But over the last decade or so, campaigns have increasingly ignored this advice, shifting their focus from converting undecided swing voters to mobilizing their base (Fiorina 1999; Goldstein and Ridout 2002). No campaign has made this shift more evident than President Bush's 2004 reelection campaign, where unprecedented amounts of money were spent trying to maximize turnout among the Republican Party faithful (Edsall 2006a).

Sorting partially accounts for this shift in campaign strategy.[9] As more voters are sorted, the size of each party's base increases. With a larger base, the marginal return on mobilizing the committed increases relative to the return on converting swing voters. The parties can therefore shift resources and effort from swing voter conversion to base mobilization as the electorate sorts.[10] While parties still work to get the swing voter to jump off the fence and onto their side, they now also devote considerable time to rallying the faithful as well.

The increase in sorting also helps to explain why high levels of elite polarization can persist. Obviously, sorting cannot explain why elites initially polarized, since elite polarization causes sorting. But once voters have sorted, the distribution of ideology within each party becomes more homogeneously liberal or conservative. Elites then face a new pressure from their partisan constituents to maintain less centrist, and more reliably liberal or conservative, positions. So while sorting is elite driven, a better-sorted electorate also has important consequences for elite behavior (on this point of mass-elite feedback loops, see McCarty, Poole, and Rosenthal 2006).

Sorting also challenges the conventional understanding of the implications of elite polarization. Most academics and pundits alike view elite polarization as a threat to the health of American democracy (Fiorina, Abrams, and Pope 2005; McCarty, Poole, and Rosenthal 2006; Binder 2008).[11] My results demonstrate that the electoral ramifications of elite polarization are not so grim—elite polarization helps voters figure out "what goes with what" and allows them to make sense of the political world. In turn, this suggests an irony underlying efforts to move away from a polarized politics (Galston and Nivola 2008): if we returned to the ideologically heterogeneous elites that characterized politics during the 1960s and 1970s, then ordinary voters would most likely struggle to make sense of the political world, just as they did during that era. There is a correlation between parties that offer voters clear and distinct policy alternatives—polarized parties (or, to use the older term, "responsible" parties; see Rae 2007)—and the extent to which citizens are able to make sense of the political world.

Finally, sorting also throws into stark relief two aspects of contemporary participatory democracy. On the one hand, we encourage citizens to be deeply and enthusiastically engaged with the political process. Yet at the same time, we also ask them to set aside their partisan convictions when they do so. My results demonstrate that these two goals are fundamentally in conflict with one another. Sorting helps voters to engage with the political process, but it also makes them more partisan. Given the role that political parties play in modern American democracy, it is effectively impossible to engage citizens in the democratic process without stoking their partisan passions—a more participatory politics is also a more partisan politics.

Overall, then, while sorting changes voter behavior, it has implications far beyond the ballot box. Sorting changes how voters behave, but it also impacts elite strategy and sheds new light on a variety of theoretical debates in American politics. Simply put, sorting has reshaped the American political landscape.

Outline of the Book

In the remainder of this book, I provide theoretical and empirical evidence in support of sorting. In chapter 2 I articulate the causal mechanism connecting elite polarization to voter sorting. As elites polarize, they send voters an increasingly clear cue about where the national parties stand on the issues of the day. This clearer signal, in turn, allow ordinary voters to align their own party and ideology.

I then provide the empirical evidence to support this theory in chapters 3–5. In chapter 3, I demonstrate that voters have sorted on a variety of different indicators of ideology. Sorting is connected to changing levels of elite polarization, and it is also a widespread, national phenomenon not confined simply to one issue, region, or birth cohort. The data presented in chapter 3 also verify that, while there has been a large increase in voter sorting, the corresponding increase in voter polarization is quite limited.

Further, the data demonstrate that the observed increase in mass polarization is due to voter sorting. So both sides of the polarization debate are partially correct: while there has been an increase in polarization—and it is due to sorting—that increase has been fairly limited.[12]

I test my elite polarization theory against other competing hypotheses in chapter 4, using both cross-sectional and panel data. I find strong support for elite polarization as a key determinant of sorting. In chapter 5 I move beyond simple claims of association to provide causal evidence connecting elite polarization and mass sorting by using data from original randomized experiments.

After establishing *why* voters sort in chapters 2–5, I take a closer look at *how* voters sort in chapter 6. There are two different paths respondents can take to move from being not sorted to sorted: they can move their partisanship into alignment with their ideology, or they can move their ideology into alignment with their partisanship. I demonstrate that sorting predominantly occurs because individuals adjust their ideology to accommodate their partisanship. Fairly unique circumstances, such as substantial elite realignment, are needed for large numbers of individuals to exit their party as a result of their ideological beliefs.

I conclude by elucidating the implications of sorting in chapter 7. I first demonstrate the large effect of sorting on voter behavior. When voters move from unsorted to sorted, they become much more likely to vote for their party's candidates, to have stronger liking for their own party and its leaders, and to bring their other issue positions into greater alignment with their party's positions. This sorting-driven shift fundamentally changes the candidates' electoral calculus and partially explains the shift from conversion- to mobilization-driven campaigns, as well as other patterns of elite behavior. I also discuss how sorting offers new insights into the debates over participatory democracy and how sorting offers an alternative perspective on the consequences of elite polarization. In this concluding chapter I demonstrate how sorting has reshaped the electoral landscape of American politics.

CHAPTER TWO

Why Voters Sort

In the previous chapter I argued that elite polarization drives sorting but did not fully specify the mechanism by which this process occurs. Elite polarization clarifies where the parties stand on the issues of the day. As elites pull apart ideologically, ordinary voters can more easily discern what positions Democrats and Republicans take. Ordinary voters then use this information to align their own partisanship and ideology: that is, they use this information to sort. Elite polarization, by clarifying where the parties stand on the issues, generates mass sorting. Figure 2.1 gives a graphical depiction of this theory. In the remainder of this chapter I will expand upon and elaborate the steps in this causal mechanism and develop the key hypotheses to be tested in later chapters.

Polarized Parties, Clearer Cues

Elite polarization clarifies the positions parties take on the issues of the day through two mechanisms. First, elite polarization increases the ideological distance between the parties—Democrats' positions become more distinct from their Republican opponents' positions. Voters look to elites who share their values to figure out where they should stand on the issues (Zaller 1992; Brody 1991). When both parties take very similar positions on an issue, aligning one's partisanship and issue position is quite compli-

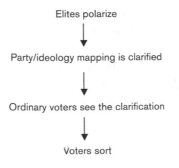

Elites polarize

Party/ideology mapping is clarified

Ordinary voters see the clarification

Voters sort

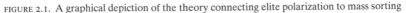

FIGURE 2.1. A graphical depiction of the theory connecting elite polarization to mass sorting

cated. But when the parties take more distinct positions, this cue-taking process is much simpler. Distinct elite positions mean clear and simple elite cues: Democrats stand for X, Republicans stand for Y, and X and Y are different positions. These clearer elite cues in turn generate sorting: voters can more easily adopt their party's position or change their party affiliation to fit with their view of the issue.

To illustrate this point, consider the scenario faced by voters trying to align their partisanship and their position on abortion at two different points in time: in the early 1970s and in the late 1990s. In the early 1970s, both parties took ambiguous positions on the issue, without any clear separation of the parties even at the elite level (Adams 1997; Stimson 2004). It would have been quite difficult for an ordinary voter to deduce what his party's position on abortion was (or which party supported his position on abortion). But if we fast-forward twenty-five years to the late 1990s, it is very clear where each party stands on abortion: elite Democrats are predominantly pro-choice, and elite Republicans are predominantly pro-life (Adams 1997). Given the sharp elite polarization on this issue, ordinary voters can infer where each party stands on the issue, which allows them to match their partisanship with their position on abortion.

This same process operates not only on abortion but across a range of issues more generally. Elites have become polarized across a host of issues, not simply one or two (though they are almost certainly more polarized in some areas than in others). As a result, in the contemporary political environment, the party labels have become "brand names," each standing for a distinct set of ideological positions (Aldrich 1995; Cox and McCubbins 1993; Snyder and Ting 2002; Tomz and Sniderman 2005).[1] In this scenario, when party labels align with ideology and are quite informative, voters should have much less trouble aligning their partisanship and beliefs than when the elite parties take more muddled positions.

Second, elite polarization also makes each party more ideologically homogeneous, which further simplifies the cue-taking process.[2] As the parties pull apart on an issue, each party becomes increasingly identified with a "side" of the issue—for example, Democrats are more supportive of expanding the rights of gay and lesbian Americans and Republicans are more supportive of tax cuts. Once the parties have staked out a position, fewer politicians with the minority view join the party, at least if they hope to one day rise to positions of prominence (Stimson 2004). Primary elections also further accelerate this process of homogenization. A candidate who takes a position at odds with the majority of her party's voters is vulnerable to a challenger with the more popular position. For example, a pro-life challenger to a pro-choice Republican incumbent is well poised to exploit the fact that the incumbent is out of step with her primary electorate (Brady, Han, and Pope 2007). This drives heterodox politicians from the parties over time, yielding greater within-party agreement on the issues (Stimson 2004).

This increasing within-party homogeneity reduces the variance of elite cues coming from the party. When elites are divided on an issue—say Democrats on civil rights in the 1960s—which part of the party determines the signal? Was the Democratic Party the party of northern liberals fighting for civil rights like Paul Douglas and Hubert Humphrey? Or were Democrats defined by the southern segregation supporters like James Eastland and Strom Thurmond? What was the position of "the party?" The answer was unclear. But thirty years later, when the Democrats no longer had a southern segregationist wing, the party's position on civil rights issues *was* clear: the Democrats were the pro–civil rights party. By the 1990s, the cue on civil rights issues was much more homogeneous than it had been a generation before. As a result, ordinary voters got one signal from the party in lieu of two, which greatly simplified the cue-taking process.

The logic here parallels Zaller's 1992 discussion of one-sided versus two-sided information flows. In a two-sided information flow (e.g., the Democratic Party on civil rights in the 1950s or either party on abortion policy in the 1970s), party elites are divided on an issue, so the mass public will also be divided (see Zaller 1992, chap. 9). Internally divided elite parties produce divided mass parties (Gabel and Scheve 2007). But when parties are unified, the situation is more akin to Zaller's one-sided model (e.g., Republicans on the president's Social Security privatization plan in 2005 or on the Bush tax cuts in 2001), and as a result, the mass party is likewise more unified (see also Wagner 2007). A more unified elite party, then, should produce a more well-sorted mass party.

Comparative studies of voter ideology also indirectly offers some support for this theoretical mechanism. A number of studies have shown that ideological thinking is somewhat weaker in the United States than in Western European nations (Barnes et al. 1979; Fuchs and Klingemann 1990; Niemi and Westholm 1984). This literature, however, overlooks the endogeneity of ideological thinking (Sniderman and Levendusky 2007). When elites offer voters stark, ideological choices—which they did to a greater extent in Western Europe than in the United States, at least in the 1970s and 1980s—voters will think in more ideological terms. When elites "package" politics in ideological terms, voters will display more understanding of ideological concepts (Hinich and Munger 1997; Freire 2008). In order for voters to be sorted, they need elites to present them with more clearly defined ideological alternatives. Elite polarization—by increasing the ideological differences between the parties and decreasing the differences within each party—provides such a mechanism.

But there is an important caveat to this discussion of the role of elite polarization: not all voters will sort in response to elite polarization. In particular, only those who actually recognize that the parties have changed their positions will sort. If citizens do not realize that the Democratic and Republican parties now provide more distinctive cues about how party and issue positions align, then there is little reason to expect those citizens to be sorted. Given this, I expect only those citizens who actually recognize that elites have diverged and consequently have clarified their positions to be able to align their own party and ideology (see also Layman and Carsey 2002b).

The Source of Elite Cues

I argue above that voters use elite cues to sort, but this claim in turn generates another question: where do these elite cues originate? Which elites define where "the party" stands on the issues? I argue that two sets of actors determine where the party stands on the issues for the mass public: the president (or presidential nominees) and members of Congress. First, and most importantly, voters look to the positions taken by the presidential candidates during the quadrennial presidential elections. The presidential nominee has to reconcile the differences between the various factions within each party and thus is perhaps the only person who can claim to speak for "the party" (Sanbonmatsu 2002). As a result, his or her positions typically become the party's positions in the eyes of the electorate.

Second, the public also looks to the parties' congressional delegations. Voters need to learn two pieces of information about where the parties stand on a given issue: the ideological distance between the parties (how far apart are Democrats and Republicans on this issue?) and the ideological homogeneity within each party (how similar are Democrats [Republicans] to one another on this issue?). Because the presidential nominee is only one individual, he or she cannot provide any information about the diversity of views within the party. But because there are several hundred members of Congress, the congressional delegation provides voters with a means of assessing opinion heterogeneity within the parties.

There is considerable evidence that voters do in fact look to members of Congress to see where the party stands on the issues. Voters absorb the aggregate roll call record of the parties and use this to make relatively informed judgments about the parties' issue positions (Cox and McCubbins 1993; Aldrich 1995; Snyder and Ting 2002; Woon and Pope 2008). There is even some evidence that voters can (relatively) accurately assess the degree of heterogeneity within each party (Pope and Woon 2007). Although voters do not follow each roll call vote carefully, they do seem to learn where the parties stand (generally speaking) on salient issues.

This explains *to whom* voters turn to learn the elite positions. But *how* do they learn these positions? Voters use a combination of five general mechanisms to learn where the parties stand on the issues of the day. First, and most importantly, there are the campaigns themselves. During the election season, news and advertisements about the candidates saturate the airwaves, and voters are bombarded with position-specific information from politicians (Franz et al. 2007). One does not have to be a political junkie to find out information about the candidates during an election—it is almost impossible not to. Ordinary voters consequently have fairly accurate views about where the parties stand on salient issues, at least at the presidential level (Gilens, Vavreck, and Cohen 2007).

Second, even outside the campaign context, strategic politicians work to ensure that their issue positions are disseminated to the mass public. Politicians are constantly searching for an advantage over the other side.

As a result, they broadcast the issues where they and their party are strongest (the theory of "issue ownership"; see Petrocik 1996; Druckman, Jacobs, and Ostermeier 2004), and they reframe issues where they are weak (Riker 1986; Schattschneider 1960).[3] Citizens need not follow politics carefully to see these messages—elites are not trying to be particularly subtle. For example, in the 1980s, voters did not need to carefully compare the parties' platforms and position papers to know that the Republicans were tougher on crime—Republicans broadcast this message loudly and clearly in their rhetoric (Carmines, Gerrity and Wagner 2005; Lin 1998). Politicians will strategically highlight their party's record—as well as their opponent's—on issues where they perceive it to be advantageous to do so. As a result, voters will see messages about the party positions in advertising, campaign materials, and media accounts, even if they only pay cursory attention to politics.

Third, (informal) party activists also serve as a mechanism for transmitting information about where the elite parties stand to ordinary voters. This is the classic "two-step" information flow model. Elites first send out cues about their positions on the issues, and attentive voters—the informal activists—notice these cues and update their beliefs. These informal activists then disseminate this information to ordinary voters (Berelson, Lazarsfeld, and McPhee 1954; Carmines and Stimson 1989). So even voters who are largely disengaged from elite communications can learn where the parties stand by relying upon their more attentive friends and colleagues (see also Baumer and Gold 2007).

Fourth, and closely related to the role of activists, there is the role of interest groups and social movements. Beginning in the 1960s, many interest groups—particularly single-issue groups—became more involved with politics (Berry 1984; Brady, Han, and Pope 2007). Although many of these groups initially worked with both parties, over time they all gradually became aligned with one party or the other (Sinclair 2006). Civil rights, environmental, gay rights, and women's groups aligned with the Democratic Party, whereas conservative Christian groups (the "Religious Right" or "Christian Right"), pro-life advocates, and low-tax groups allied with the Republican Party. Many of these groups have become key players within the parties and are heavily involved with candidate recruitment and selection (see Green 1995 for the case of the Religious Right). This group-party alignment, then, will further clarify to voters where the parties stand on the issues, especially controversial social issues. For example, once conservative Christian groups became aligned with the Republicans—and once pro-choice groups became aligned with the Democrats—this dramatically reduced the ambiguity about where the parties stood on abortion (Gerrity, Wagner, and Carmines 2004). Interest groups (and the related social movements), by attaching themselves to a party, help voters to see where the parties stand on the issues of the day.[4]

Finally, voters also get a good deal of information about politics and party positions as they go about their everyday lives—that is, through "accidental data" (Downs 1957). This type of information is not anything that people seek out per se; rather, it is simply obtained in the process of doing something else (see also Popkin 1991). For example, they might see a campaign commercial while watching *Lost* or notice a headline about the president's response to interest rate cuts while looking for the sports scores in the morning newspaper. There is a torrent of free information in our society, and while most is lost, some is absorbed, and some of what is absorbed is used to update beliefs about where the parties stand on the issues (Popkin 1991). Accidental data act as a heuristic (Sniderman, Brody, and Tetlock 1991), allowing voters to assess party positions without having to bear the high costs of becoming informed on all of them.

In turn, these various mechanisms for voter learning also highlight several important points about the connection between masses and elites. First, note that the mass media obviously lurk in the background of nearly all of these mechanisms. Here, I chose not to list the media as a separate mechanism in large part because the media transmit information about elite positions in a variety of different ways (e.g., coverage of campaigns themselves, coverage of politicians between campaigns, in "accidental data"), and I wanted to highlight these alternative mechanisms. But the reader should note that the mass media play a vital role in transmitting information about elite positions to ordinary voters.

Further, even independent of these particular mechanisms, as elites become more polarized, the media should reflect this polarization (Mutz 2006). This prediction comes from indexing theory (Bennett 1990), which argues that news reporting reflects the ideological balance of competing elites. So when political leaders take centrist, consensual positions on an issue, news stories on that topic will emphasize these centrist positions. By contrast, when elites are more divided and polarized, the news reporting will reflect these more polarized stances (see also Hallin 1984). So as elites have polarized over the past thirty years, discussions of politics in the media should reflect this increasing polarization. As elites themselves become more polarized, the media coverage should reflect this change.

It should also be clear that voters do *not* acquire in-depth assessments of the parties' positions from any of these activities. Rather, they learn a crude summary of where the parties stand on the issues: Democrats are more supportive of abortion rights, Republicans will be tougher on the Soviet Union, and the like. Voters do not deal in subtlety; they deal in simplicity: which party is more liberal, and whether the parties are united or divided on an issue. This observation is not meant to be derisive but rather is meant to reflect the gut-level rationality that characterizes voter decision making (Popkin 1991). However, as I will demonstrate in later chapters, even this relatively basic information about elites can exert a powerful influence on citizens' behavior.

This in turn explains why elites repeat their messages so frequently over time. Because voters pay only sporadic attention to politics, and glean only a basic message from what elites say, they will need to hear repeated messages from elites. It will not simply be enough for elites to change their position subtly and say it once—they will need to repeatedly state a point over and over again for the electorate to update their beliefs (see also (Tomz and Sniderman 2005). Further, the fact that the parties have existed for over a century gives them a history with most voters. Voters do not think the parties can change overnight, so repetition is needed to ensure that voters know elites' positions actually have changed. Because they are not sophisticated Bayesian updaters, citizens' beliefs about the parties will change slowly in response to variations in elite positions.

This dynamic also generates an important prediction for empirical tests of my sorting theory. First, given this need for repetition, in most circumstances there will be a lag between elite-level changes and mass response. Voters will update, but they will do it slowly, thereby generating a lag. My theory does not give any predictions about the length of this lag, but it is clear it typically will exist. But there is also an important caveat to this general rule. Certain elite events dramatically shift the signal parties send to voters, and as a result, voters will not need to see as much repetition. In these cases, I expect to see a more marked increase in sorting following this type of elite clarification. So, for example, I expect to find a large increase in sorting following the 1994 Republican takeover of the House or following the debate over the Iraq War during the Bush administration. So while a lag between elite action and mass reaction typically exists, dramatic elite shifts should produce more rapid voter responses. This also implies that increases in sorting will occur primarily in response to fairly dramatic events.

Finally, changes in party competition over time will alter the salience of various issues. As an issue rises in prominence, there will be more discussion and debate about it at the elite level. As a result, voters will generally find it easier to discern where the parties stand, which should in turn increase sorting (Goren and Delancey 2008). This sort of variation in salience may help to explain variation in sorting *across* issues at any given point in time.[5]

The Role of Media Changes

I discussed above how the media—by covering campaigns and other political events—help ordinary voters to learn where the parties stand on the issues. While this is an important piece of the puzzle, it leaves out a key development from the past few years: the dramatic reshaping of the "post-broadcast" media environment, in particular, the fragmentation of the media environment in the Internet age (Prior 2007). Have any of these changes contributed to sorting? In particular, have any media changes made it easier for ordinary voters to learn where the parties stand on the issues?

I hypothesize that two particular media changes should increase sorting (by making it easier for voters to learn the parties' positions). First, there is now much more media choice than thirty—or even ten—years ago (Prior 2007; see also Hamilton 2003). A generation ago, there were only a few major networks, but in the ensuing decades, the Internet, podcasts, talk radio, blogs, chat rooms, and the like have opened up a whole new world of news. So today, for political junkies, there is an almost nonstop barrage of news and information. If voters choose to consume it, political media are available around the clock, which should simplify the process of learning the parties' positions.[6]

Second, as a consequences of this increased media choice, there has been an increase in narrowcasting, where programmers tailor their content to the partisan and ideological disposition of their audience (Mutz 2006; Prior 2007). There are liberal and conservative outlets, and they each give their own distinct slant to the news and current events. Patterns of selective exposure to media content magnify the effect of this trend. Despite the proliferation of media outlets in recent years, Americans increasingly sample only a small number of them—those that fit with their existing partisan or ideological orientations (Iyengar and Hahn 2007).

This promotes an "echo chamber" effect, whereby voters hear their side's message over and over again (Stroud 2008; Kernell and Rice 2008; Iyengar et al. 2008). Voters who consume these sorts of programs should therefore find themselves inundated with partisan cues from their side of the aisle, which should heighten their awareness of party positions.[7]

Both of these changes in the media environment should make it easier for voters to learn where the parties stand on the issues of the day, which in turn should increase sorting. But at the same time, a number of counter-trends exist that may limit the impact of these changes for most Americans (Rosensteil 2006). Most importantly, many Americans consume little or no political media: despite the increase in available options, they still get most of their information from the major TV networks, or even from "soft" news sources (Baum 2005). These mainstream sources are less partisan, and voters may need to pay closer attention to discern the parties' positions on the issues. Further, many American also consume multiple sources of news and information, not all of which share the same (or even any) partisan bias. As a result, the effect of media changes on sorting may be less dramatic than it appears at first glance.

There are also other patterns that may have an unclear effect on the media's role in transmitting information on party positions. For example, media coverage of politics and elections has become increasingly negative (Cappella and Jamieson 1997; Patterson 1994). This increases public cynicism toward politics (Cappella and Jamieson 1997) and therefore might make the public less likely to be receptive to any partisan messages. Alternatively, it might delegitimize only the opposition, making it more likely that voters tune out only the other side. Ultimately, careful research will be needed to parse out these competing hypotheses.

All of this suggests that the role of media changes in the sorting process is too complex to tease out in only a few pages. While I offer evidence below demonstrating that the media writ large play a role in sorting, I leave it for future scholars to document how recent media changes have affected the sorting process.

Measuring the Elite Policy Positions

Now that I know what actors define the parties' positions and how those positions are transmitted to voters, I need to actually measure the positions over time. To do this, I focus on the positions of the presidential nominees and members of Congress, since they are the key actors who shape the public's perception of the parties' positions. In particular, I look at important campaign documents and news coverage of elite behavior to determine what positions the parties take on the issues and how those positions change over time. I also supplement this analysis with a coding of media sources to analyze the ways in which the mass media have transmitted information about the positions taken by political elites over time. Doing so will allow me to draw inferences about the clarity of the cues voters have received over time.

Ideally, I would also have systematic data on the alignment of parties and interest groups, the attitudes of issue activists, and the types of "free information" voters get as they go about their daily lives. Unfortunately, data on these sources do not really exist, particularly for the interest groups and "free information" (indeed, it is unclear how to even systematically measure the latter).[8] As a result, the picture I paint below will necessarily be limited, though not in a debilitating way. The trends in the party positions will be relatively clear and straightforward, and though having this additional data would be helpful, I ultimately will not need it to tell my story.

I rely on several sources of information to measure the parties' positions and how they have changed over time. First, for the positions taken by the presidential candidates, I code the issues each candidate discussed in his acceptance speech at the party convention, and I supplement this with an analysis of campaign coverage in *CQ Weekly Report* (later, *CQ Weekly*). I do a similar qualitative coding of the party platforms to provide additional information about where the parties stand on the issues. The argument is not that people actually read the party platforms: they do not. Rather, it is simply that the platform highlights some of the issues important to the party and the nominee (Sanbonmatsu 2002).[9] Taken together, these sources will give an excellent overview of where the nominees stood on the key issues over time.

To describe the signal sent by members of Congress, I primarily rely on a similar coding of secondary sources analyzing congressional behavior. This allows me to assess how congressional behavior—particularly heterogeneity in congressional behavior—translates into the signals sent to citizens. As a whole, this summary of the party positions will allow me to capture the parties' positions, and how they have changed, over time.[10]

To supplement this campaign analysis, I also examined the media's portrayal of elite positions over time. In particular, I examined how the mainstream media discussed congressional polarization over time: do the media discuss the growing ideological divide between the parties? This media analysis allows me to verify that even citizens who are inattentive to campaigns themselves, and learn about politics only via the media, can and do receive information about elite positions and polarization.

Over-Time Variation in the Elite Ideological Signals

During the 1950s and 1960s, most candidates of both parties largely accepted the postwar New Deal consensus—those decades are remarkable for the degree of bipartisanship and commonality between the parties (Han and Brady 2007). Yet that began to change in the mid-1960s with the nomination of Barry Goldwater, the first candidate to explicitly reject much of the postwar liberalism, advocating the privatization of Social Security, the sale of the Tennessee Valley Authority, and the strengthening of the right-to-work laws (Baer 2000, 17). Indeed, the Goldwater campaign and its discussion of civil rights as a states' rights issue helped to split the parties over the question of race (Carmines and Stimson 1989). This was the first signal to voters that change was brewing in the party system.

In the early 1970s, the McGovern-Fraser reforms opened up the Democratic Party's primary process, decentralizing power from the party bosses to the passionate and active who vote in the party's primaries and caucuses; the Republican Party would eventually follow suit (Perlstein 2008; Cohen et al. 2008). This sea change in the nomination process altered the calculus of a candidate seeking the nomination. A nominee now needs to stake out more ideologically extreme positions on the issues to capture the support of activists, who want to win elections but also value maintaining ideological purity. Given the rise of new, politically active social movements during the late 1960s (Brady, Han, and Pope 2007), this sort of calculation became even more important. This pressure to take more noncentrist positions helps to clarify the ideological location of the parties, as I discuss below in the context of the Reagan era.

The 1972 nomination of Senator George McGovern on the Democratic ticket certainly marked a high point of postwar liberalism. McGovern embraced a variety of economically liberal positions involving considerable government intervention into the marketplace: he suggested that the federal government guarantee each citizen a basic income and a job, fully fund national health insurance, and so on. McGovern, lacking some of the support of traditional Democratic allies like labor unions, embraced the "new left," the antiwar and student protesters, which was reflected in his stances on Vietnam and various social issues (Layman 2001; Perlstein 2008; Miroff 2007). Indeed, McGovern held the strongest dove position (immediate withdrawal) on the Vietnam War, one of the most contentious issues of the day, promising a complete withdrawal from Southeast Asia within ninety days of his inauguration.[11] And McGovern also took somewhat-liberal stances on the cultural issues of the day, supporting gun control, busing as a means of achieving school integration, and so forth (Baer 2000). Not only was McGovern to the left economically, but he also took sharply liberal positions on foreign-policy, racial, and cultural issues. There could be little doubt about the ideological signal sent by McGovern in 1972.

Nixon's policies, by contrast, were not so easily categorized. On the one hand, he did espouse a number of conservative positions. His famous "Southern Strategy"—combining appeals to economic conservatism with a "tough on crime" message—cast him as the conservative candidate in the race (Black and Black 2002, 210–211). As part of his appeal to the South, Nixon took a conservative stand on matters of racial policy. While McGovern supported busing schoolchildren across district lines, Nixon took a more conservative approach, promising to ease measures aimed at desegregation (Carmines and Stimson 1989, 54). At the same time, Nixon broke with conservative orthodoxy on other issues. For example, he introduced and defended wage and price controls, a level of intrusion into the market almost unthinkable in elite Republican circles after the rise of supply-side economics in the 1980s (Sinclair 2006; Smith 2007). Additionally, Nixon also garnered some support from liberal Republican groups (Rae 1989). While there was little ambiguity about McGovern's stands, Nixon did not embrace conservative orthodoxy to the same extent that later Republican nominees would.

But even if the nominees and activists were beginning to clarify the party positions in the early 1970s, the congressional delegations of both parties at that time remained fairly heterogeneous. So most citizens, regardless of party or ideology, could point to some congresspeople who shared their party and ideology. In particular, no doubt Democrats to the right of McGovern could find other party leaders who took views more in line with their own. Given this sort of muted ideological signal from the parties, we would not expect to see many mismatched partisans (liberal Republicans and conservative Democrats) changing their ideology or partisanship—by and large, the elite cue they received was still somewhat ambiguous.

The Reagan Years

Reagan's campaign and election contributed to the ideological gulf between the parties. While McGovern failed to move his party to the left, Reagan succeeded at moving the Republican Party to the right. Reagan's election was the culmination of twenty years of work by the conservative networks established during the Goldwater campaign (Perlstein 2001). Under Reagan, unabashedly conservative positions become more accepted in the Republican Party: across-the-board reductions in tax rates to spur economic growth (and an embrace of supply-side economics), devolution of policies like welfare back to the states, and a strong posture vis-à-vis the Soviet Union. All of these issue positions gave voters a clear signal about where the Republican Party stood.

Carter's 1980 campaign took a more liberal stance on many of these items: criticizing the Reagan defense plan as likely to spur an arms race, increasing the federal role in social programs like welfare, and so on. Indeed, the Democratic platform stressed the need for a strong federal government and the need for détente with the USSR, standing in stark contrast to Reagan's relatively antigovernment, promarket rhetoric and clearly distinguishing the signal sent by the parties to voters. The 1984 campaign, pitting Reagan, advocating a continuation of the above conservative policies, against Mondale, advocating a softer approach to the USSR, a nuclear freeze, increased taxes, and so on, again gave voters a clear signal about the parties' relative positions.

Once in office, Reagan's policies on defense spending, tax cuts, and various domestic spending programs sharply divided the nation's elite along ideological lines (Abramowitz and Saunders 1998, 636–637). The Reagan administration also moved to slow the pace of civil rights reforms, clarifying that the party took a more conservative position here as well (Carmines and Stimson 1989, 54). Additionally, conservative Democratic and liberal Republican legislators found themselves frequently cross-pressured—due in part to leadership strategies (Sinclair 1995) and other tactics (Roberts and Smith 2003)—and began exiting the scene either by defeat or by retirement (see also Sinclair 2006), further homogenizing the party cues.

Reagan and his advisors also adopted conservative positions on social issues in an effort to woo religious voters. Although it may be hard to recall this in today's political environment, until a generation ago evangelicals did not think religion and politics should mix. Throughout the 1960s and early 1970s, evangelicals and other conservative religious leaders felt their mission was to focus on the next world, not this one. Jerry Falwell—later the founder of the Moral Majority, one of the important early "Religious Right" groups—noted in 1965: "We have few ties to this earth. . . . Believing in the Bible as I do, I would find it impossible to stop preaching the pure saving Gospel of Jesus Christ and begin doing anything else, including fighting communism or participating in civil rights reforms. . . . Preachers are not called upon to be politicians but to be soul winners. Nowhere are we commissioned to reform the externals."[12] There is nothing inevitable about evangelicals participating in politics and, in particular, nothing inevitable about their participation in Republican politics: recall that evangelicals voted predominantly for Carter in 1976 (Layman 2001). Strategic elites would be needed to capture the allegiance of religious voters.

The social turmoil and changing mores of the 1960s and 1970s gave the political operatives a way to recruit evangelical leaders—and their congregations—to the Republican flock. The Supreme Court's decisions on school prayer and abortion, combined with the women's movement and the new permissiveness of popular culture, convinced evangelicals that they could no longer stay removed from politics: they needed to enter the fray on behalf of traditional values and to combat the secularization of America (Sinclair 2006). But even so, evangelical participation was not guaranteed—strategic Republican elites worked closely with key figures like Falwell and Pat Robertson to bring them (and their flocks) into the Republican fold (Layman 2001; Sinclair 2006).[13]

The party platforms began to reflect these newly divisive stands on social issues. Abortion policy provides a particularly stark case. Both parties took fairly muted stands on abortion in their respective party platforms during the 1970s but began to diverge in the 1980s. For example, the 1980 Democratic platform commented: "The Democratic Party supports the 1973 Supreme Court decision on abortion rights as the law of the land and opposes any constitutional amendment to restrict or overturn that decision." By 1988, the position had veered further to the left: "the fundamental right of reproductive choice should be guaranteed regardless of the ability to pay." By the late 1980s, for Democrats, the position on abortion was clear: it was a "fundamental right" of all Americans. The Republican Party position underwent a similar clarifying process, though the Republican position was more firmly pro-life by 1980. Movement by strategic politicians helped drive the parties farther apart on abortion.

This move toward clarity is true not only for abortion but also for other cultural issues like school prayer, gay rights, the death penalty, and so forth. Reagan's rhetoric and polices on social issues made it clear that the Republican Party had chosen to join forces with the Christian Right. In his 1984 acceptance speech, Reagan remarked: "If our opponents were as vigorous in supporting our voluntary prayer amendment as they are in raising taxes, maybe we could get the Lord back into schoolrooms and drugs and violence out."[14] The parties moved apart during the 1980s and 1990s as strategic politicians transformed American politics by bringing these new issues—and the new voters and activists they mobilized—from the sidelines to the forefront (Layman 2001).

The Bush-Dukakis contest continued these same patterns. Bush positioned himself as the heir to the conservative Reagan legacy: peace through strength and security, a strong approach to the USSR, a pledge to not raise taxes (the famous "read my lips" promise), and a calculated (and effective) strategy to paint Dukakis as a liberal out of touch with mainstream values, emphasizing his record on issues like prison furloughs, gun control, and the death penalty (Elving 1988). Although Dukakis famously claimed that this "election is about competence, not ideology," he could not escape being tarred by the "L" word (liberal). Throughout the 1980s, Republicans succeeded in moving their party to the right on a variety of issues like defense, taxes and spending, the death penalty, and crime. At the same time, these Republican elites were also able to paint the Democratic candidates as being too liberal on this same constellation of issues. The relative positions of the political parties was fairly clear by the mid- to late 1980s.

Clinton and the Politics of the 1990s

Clinton, by contrast, pulled the Democratic Party toward the center in 1992. Although he promised to raise taxes on those earning over $200,000 a year and enact universal health care, he also moderated the party's position on abortion (his famous argument that abortion should be safe, legal, and rare) and other issues such as law and order, advocating an increase in police forces. After the 1994 elections, when his liberal policies (such as the health care effort, the assault weapons ban, and the tax hike) led many in his party to defeat (Brady et al. 1996), Clinton moderated further in 1996, reforming welfare, declaring "the era of big government is over," and stressing tax cuts for college education, school uniforms, the banning of cop-killer bullets, and other less controversial, more moderate policies.

Crime policy provides a specific example of Clinton's centrism. Throughout the 1960s, 1970s, and 1980s, Democrats were considered by many to be soft on crime, more concerned with protecting the rights of the accused than the rights of crime victims. Republicans began to emphasize "law-and-order" themes in their campaigns, beginning with Goldwater, and the public responded by viewing Republicans as more adept on crime. However, Clinton changed the dynamics of the crime issue by redefining it, making it about gun control and putting more police on the streets. Further, Clinton visibly challenged traditional Democratic elites over their support for the civil liberties of the accused. Together, these actions made crime policy a real, viable issue for Democratic candidates (Lin 1998). The public responded by seeing the Democrats as more capable stewards on law-and-order issues (Carmines, Gerrity, and Wagner 2005). By moving the party away from traditional Democratic groups (the accused), Clinton was able to articulate a more centrist policy for the Democrats.

The Republican Party continued to advocate conservative policies on both economic and social issues. The 1994 Republican takeover of the House and the "Contract with America" shifted the party's image dramatically to the right on a whole host of issues from gun control to taxes and spending to social issues. At the same time, the presidential nominees (Bush and Dole) both pushed conservative policies on economic, racial, and social issues, emphasizing limited government intrusion into the economy and a return to more traditional cultural mores. During the 1996 campaign, Bob Dole stressed the Republican position on smaller, low-tax government, emphasizing themes of economic freedom (smaller government, lower taxes, etc.) and personal responsibility that have been party mainstays for the past two decades (see Gerring 1998).

The Republican takeover of the House also marked a major turning point for the alignment of interest groups with the parties. While the Democratic leadership had begun to coordinate with groups formally in the late 1980s, the Republican victory in 1994 ushered in a whole new era of group-party relations. The Republicans formed the "Thursday Club," which allowed key groups (e.g., Christian Right organizations, the National Rifle Association, Americans for Tax Reform, the National Federation of Independent Business, and other stakeholder groups) to meet with

Republican leaders and discuss policy (Sinclair 2006). This sort of alignment—and direct group involvement in the process—further clarified the parties' positions, most notably by helping to drive apart the policy positions advanced by the parties. So, for example, once the NRA had a formal voice in the Republican agenda, there could be little ambiguity about where the parties stood on gun control. Interest group giving strategies after the 1994 election further tightened this group-party linkage. Traditionally, most groups had given money primarily to incumbents from both parties as a strategy of buying access to members of Congress. But after 1994, more groups adopted a "partisan" strategy, whereby they gave primarily to one party or the other (Wand 2007; see also Rae 2007). As these groups aligned themselves with the parties, the positions espoused by the parties became clearer, and ordinary voters could more easily discern where the national parties stood on the issues of the day.

The 1990s also saw one of the most dramatic modern examples of political scandal, the Lewinsky affair, culminating in the impeachment of the president. The intense partisan divisions on display in the Congress during the trial—particularly the Republican push for impeachment when large segments of the general public favored a less severe option, such as censure—again highlighted the ideological differences between the parties.

George W. Bush and the Twenty-first Century

In 2000, George W. Bush adopted the Clinton strategy and moved the Republicans in a centrist direction with his message of "compassionate conservatism," pledging to be a "uniter, not a divider." Bush emphasized his record of bipartisanship as governor of Texas and his strong support for education in an effort to move the public's perception of the party away from the harsh image projected by the Republican Congress (Edsall 2006b). Gore, on the other hand, framed his campaign in terms of "the people versus the powerful," a liberal populist message that emphasized fighting entrenched interests like big business with the power of government. Survey data demonstrate that, as a result, voters perceived Gore to be one of the most liberal candidates for president of the past generation, more outside the mainstream than Bush (Fiorina, Abrams, and Pope 2003).

By 2004, after the Bush tax cuts, debates over drilling in the Alaska National Wildlife Refuge, and the Iraq War, it was fairly evident that

Bush was conservative. Even casual observers knew that Bush—with his justifications for preemption abroad, limiting civil liberties at home, and so forth—was firmly to the right. Likewise, Kerry's policies, and his long liberal Senate voting record, identified him as being firmly on the left (Clinton, Jackman, and Rivers 2004).[15]

The proposed constitutional amendment banning same-sex marriage also supplied another high-profile division between the parties on a social issue. While earlier platforms had discussed gay/lesbian issues, they had been at only the periphery of the debate before 2004. With the parties taking opposite positions on the proposed constitutional amendment banning same-sex marriage, voters again received a clear signal on where the parties stood on social issues. By 2004, regardless of the issue—social, economic, civil rights, foreign policy—the signals about the locations of the two major parties were fairly distinct and unambiguous.

Further, the same sort of division between the two elite parties has also been mimicked at the activist level. Whereas at one time the parties' activists were more ideologically heterogeneous, today they are clearly divided into distinct ideological camps. Surveys of convention delegates show huge gaps between the activists, much larger than the parallel gaps between the mass parties (Sinclair 2006; Layman 2001; Carmines and Stimson 1989), again providing a clear signal about the relative locations of the parties.

Overall, the evidence is clear: elite party positions are now more divided than they were a generation ago. While a generation ago the parties were quite heterogeneous at the elite level, they are now much more unified and polarized. Note that these changes are not simply limited to one issue or set of issues but rather are widespread. Party polarization has grown to encompass most of the major issues on the policy agenda. Throughout this period, the parties have been divided on traditional left-right economic issues (like spending, taxes, etc.) and racial policies (such as affirmative action). Additionally, the parties have also become increasingly divided on social issues such as abortion, school prayer, and gay rights. The debate during the 2004 election also suggests that issues about foreign policy may have resurfaced as a partisan/ideological division, with Republicans taking the proactive position (Shapiro and Bloch-Elkon 2006).[16] So we now see a sharp division on nearly all dimensions relevant to American politics. On a host of issues, the Democrats take the "left" position, the Republicans take the "right" position, and there is little overlap between the two. The cues ordinary voters now receive from partisan elites—as opposed to those from four decades ago—are quite distinct.

A Caveat: The Limits of Sorting

Although the parties' positions have become much clearer since the 1970s, there is an important limitation to this argument. The parties are now more ideologically cohesive and polarized, but they also spend part of their time promoting a nonideological image. Part of what parties do to win elections is stress valence issues (like character, integrity, honesty, etc.; see Stokes 1963).[17] To the extent that parties emphasize these sorts of issues, there are limits to sorting: there is little about "honesty" or "character" that would help an individual to align his partisanship and ideological views.

And these sorts of valence appeals are part of the party repertoire. For example, when the Democratic National Committee does party-building activity, they (at least around the 2006 election season) stressed "The Democratic Vision," a six-point plan.[18] While there is some substance, it is largely valence driven: (1) Honest Leadership and Open Government, (2) Real Security, (3) Energy Independence, (4) Economic Prosperity and Educational Excellence, (5) A Health Care System That Works for Everyone, and (6) Retirement Security.[19] It is hard to imagine, for example, being against honesty, quality education, a strong economy, and security for Americans. To the extent that the parties stress these sorts of issues—honesty, character, "family values," and so forth—ordinary citizens get little information about how to align their party and their ideology. So the discussion of valence issues presents a limit to sorting. As the parties discuss valence issues more and substantive issues less, sorting should be more limited.

Media Coverage of Polarization

The preceding discussion of campaign behavior verifies that elites have become increasingly polarized over time across a wide variety of issues. To complement this analysis, I also systematically measured the amount of mass-media attention devoted to elite polarization over time. Doing so allows me to verify that the increasingly clear elite cues are actually conveyed to ordinary voters. While there are sources of information about elite polarization beyond the media (e.g., the campaigns themselves, trusted friends and neighbors, etc.; see the discussion earlier in this chapter), arguably the media constitute one of the most important sources for many voters, if not *the* most important source. Examining the media's coverage of elite polarization is therefore a key step to measuring the signal actually received by citizens. I hypothesized that there will be increased media coverage of elite polarization over time in light of the sustained ideological divergence discussed above.

I tested this hypothesis by counting the number of stories about congressional polarization in the *New York Times* between 1980 and 2004 using the full-text search capabilities of Lexis-Nexis Academic Universe. I searched for "Congress OR House OR Senate" within the same paragraph as "polarize OR polarized OR polarization," and the phrase "United States OR America" had to appear in the article as well. To avoid counting "false positives," I read each story and discarded any that were not on topic (e.g., stories about polarization in the Peruvian Congress).[20] This analysis makes two implicit assumptions. First, I assume that the positions of members of Congress serve as proxies for the positions of political elites more broadly. Obviously, the composition of political elites is significantly broader than the membership of Congress (see the discussion in chapter 1), but members of Congress are among the most visible national elites, and their positions are often used as proxies for the broader constellation of elites (see, e.g., Carmines and Stimson, 1989; McCarty, Poole, and Rosenthal 2006). Second, my approach also assumes that the coverage in the *Times* reflects the coverage in other media outlets. The *Times* is arguably the most commonly used source in media coding (Druckman and Chong 2009), so this assumption is a common one in the literature. While the *Times* is not a perfect proxy for other media sources (Woolley 2000), it does seem to (at least approximately) reflect what other mainstream outlets discuss (Baumgartner, De Boef, and Boydstun 2008; Gans 2004; Kiousis 2004; Soroka 2002).

Figure 2.2 plots the number of stories in the *Times* that discuss congressional polarization over time. To simplify the presentation, I have grouped the coverage into four-year windows corresponding to presidential administrations. Begin with the upper panel of figure 2.2. The data are unambiguous: the *Times* attention to congressional polarization increases dramatically over time. There are fewer than ten stories about polarization from 1980 through 1984, but there are more than thirty such stories between 2001 and 2004. The pattern over time parallels the one found in the qualitative analysis above: there is some mention of polarization during the Reagan era (particularly during his second term in office), followed by a sharp and dramatic rise in discussion of polarization beginning in the mid-1990s. It seems that media attention to polarization really exploded after the 1994 election and the move of Gingrich and others to

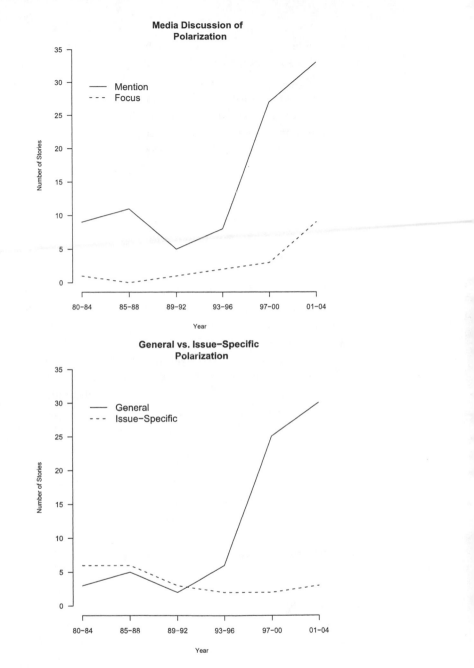

FIGURE 2.2 Counts of the number of news stories appearing in the *New York Times* about congressional polarization. The upper panel shows the number of stories discussing polarization and the number that focus specifically on congressional polarization. The lower panel shows the number of stories that discuss polarization in the context of a specific issue (e.g., polarized over aid to the Contras) and the number that discuss polarization in general.

pull the Republican Party to the right, which suggests that it may take fairly dramatic events to focus media attention on a topic like polarization.

Another indicator of increasing attention to polarization is the number of stories the *Times* publishes that are focused primarily on polarization (e.g., stories where the primary subject was elite polarization, as opposed to stories that simply discuss elite polarization in passing). While there are almost no such stories during the 1980s, there are nine such stories during George W. Bush's first term. Additionally, beginning in the late 1990s, a series of articles appeared that described the declining number of moderates in Congress, which indicates the growth of elite polarization (see, e.g., Toner 2004). All of this heightened attention to polarization should have made it easier for ordinary voters to realize that the parties' cues are now more distinctive from one another.

There is one additional wrinkle to the *Times* coverage of congressional polarization, illustrated by the lower panel of figure 2.2. In the 1980s, when the *Times* talked about polarization, it did so on an issue-specific basis. So, for example, it discussed the parties being polarized over aid to the Contras, over the budget deficit, or over arms control. But that pattern gradually shifted, and the *Times* began to discuss polarization in a more general sense. By the mid-1990s, the *Times* simply talked about polarization writ large rather than with a reference to a specific issue. Voters got a signal that elites were not simply divided over one or two specific issues but rather tended to take disparate sides across a broad spectrum of policy debates.[21]

Overall, the results of this analysis are clear: the media increasingly transmit information about congressional polarization to ordinary voters. Combined with the evidence from campaigns and campaign coverage discussed earlier, this media coverage should help voters to learn that the parties increasingly take distinct positions on the issues of the day. These clearer signals should then in turn generate additional mass sorting.

Hypotheses about Sorting

The growing ideological polarization and its connection to the behavior of ordinary voters suggest several testable hypotheses at both the micro- and the macrolevel. At the macrolevel, two hypotheses follow. First, as elites polarize, more voters should understand where the parties stand relative to one another. This tests the first step in my argument: that elite polarization clarifies the cues party elites send to voters. Second, in response to this increased awareness of elite differences, more ordinary voters should sort. This tests the second step: that with this greater awareness of party positions, voters will be more likely to align their own partisanship and ideological beliefs. Taken together, these two steps provide a strong test of my sorting argument at the macrolevel.

Likewise, there are parallel tests at the individual level. As I argued above, for an individual voter to sort, he must realize that the parties have clarified their positions. Absent this key realization, voters have little in centive to alter their beliefs (see fig. 2.1). Looking at individual-level data then, I expect to find that voters who are aware of elite divisions should be the most likely to be sorted. In the chapters that follow, I test these propositions and contrast them with other possible accounts of sorting.

Top Down or Bottom Up?

I argue throughout this book that political change begins with elites and then spreads to the masses. There are good reasons—both theoretically and empirically—to take this view. But there is another model of political change: a bottom-up model, where change begins at the mass level and filters upward to elites. While it is difficult to definitively rule out such a model as the primary determinant of sorting, I would argue that there are at least two findings that cast serious doubt on this possibility.

First, the theoretical mechanism for voters to be the driving force is quite unclear. In the elite-driven model, ordinary voters can sort because elites clarify how party and ideology relate to one another. This work builds on half a century of research demonstrating that elites are the driving force behind public opinion (Converse 1964; Carmines and Stimson 1989; Zaller 1992; Sniderman and Bullock 2004; Sniderman 2000). This should not be read to argue that ordinary citizens are fools who blindly and unquestioningly follow where elites lead—indeed, they are not (Converse 2000). Politics, however, is only a peripheral concern for most voters; hence, they need the guidance of elites to make sense of the political world. By contrast, in the bottom-up story, voters need to act *without* the aid of elites. Given the paltry amount of information about politics and public affairs possessed by ordinary voters (Delli-Carpini and Keeter 1996), it appears to ask too much of voters to make sense of politics on their own. Elites move first even on emotionally charged issues like abortion and race relations (Carmines and Stimson 1989; Adams 1997), let alone on more prosaic issues. Public opinion is an echo chamber: it reflects the inputs of elite competition, and elites are the ones doing the heavy lifting of setting the terms of the debate (Key 1966). This is not to say that it is impossible to construct a bottom-up account of sorting. It is to say, however, that a specific, plausible mechanism needs to be in place for that story to be told. Absent such a model, it is difficult to understand the structure of such a bottom-up story.

Second, the data I will present in later chapters strongly suggest that change begins with elites and then spreads to the mass public. The quantitative and qualitative data presented earlier demonstrate that, after a period of marked bipartisanship in the postwar era, elites began to diverge in the 1960s and 1970s, a process that accelerated during the 1980s, 1990s, and 2000s. To briefly preview the results from later chapters, the survey data on the mass public strongly suggest that voters have used these clearer elite cues to align their own partisanship and ideology. If the mass public was the original mover and the elites followed, then the elite parties should have become *more* heterogeneous, not less (Adams 1997). The mass public has moved precisely in the direction of the elite split, suggesting that elites are the original causal factor. The timing and amount of change in the two groups—elites begin to pull apart first, and they have pulled apart to a much greater extent than ordinary voters—strongly suggest that elites are the driving force behind sorting.

But this should not be read as a statement that I think the causal arrow can run only from elites to masses: it obviously runs in both directions. Indeed, it would be an odd conception of democratic politics if the masses never constrained elite behavior. Rather, the argument here is simply that absent very special political circumstances, ordinary voters need the help of elites to make sense of the political world. But to say such scenarios are rare is not to say they never occur. In particular, social movements and other non-elite actors do sometimes constrain elite behavior. Lee (2002) provides the most complete account of this idea. He argues that the mass protests of the civil rights era (and the social movements that generated them) influenced both mass and elite opinion (see also Chen, Mickey, and Van Houweling 2008; Feinstein and Schickler 2008). Others have told similar stories about the southern resistance to school desegregation and busing (Lassiter 2006), as well as the Lewinsky scandal (Jacobson 2006). Undoubtedly, there are complex feedback loops between ordinary voters and elites, and the "true" process of change is quite complicated (McCarty,

Poole, and Rosenthal 2006). My point is not to suggest that there is a simple linear causal story connecting masses to elites. Rather, my argument is that, at least initially, we need to begin with elites: it is hard to imagine *why* the mass public would change without some cue from elites.[22] In the concluding chapter, I discuss the ways in which a better-sorted electorate can alter elite behavior, implying that causality does run from masses to elites in some circumstances. The causal arrow is undoubtedly complex, but at the origin, generally speaking, elites move and then the masses follow.

Conclusions

This chapter explained the theoretical mechanism linking elite polarization with voter sorting. As elites polarize, they clarify where the parties stand on the issues of the day—polarized elites clarify the policy positions taken by Democrats and Republicans. Voters then use these clearer elite cues to align their own partisanship and ideology, that is, to sort. Elite polarization, then, by clarifying where the parties stand, causes voter sorting. The next step is to gather evidence to test this theory, a task I begin in the next chapter.

CHAPTER THREE

Have Voters Sorted?

In the preceding chapter I laid out my theoretical argument connecting elite polarization and voter sorting but did not provide any evidence for my theory. In this chapter I begin to provide the empirical support for my sorting theory. In particular, I focus on testing two aggregate-level predictions about sorting. First, as elites become increasingly more polarized, more voters will recognize that the elite parties take distinct positions on the issues. Second, in response to these increasingly clear elite stances, voters will sort. Verifying these hypotheses will provide the first crucial support for my argument.

To test these hypotheses, I need over-time data on the political attitudes and opinions of American voters. I use the National Election Study (NES) data, the long-standing benchmark study of the political attitudes of the American people.[1] In this chapter, I rely primarily on the NES cross-sectional studies: every two years, the NES interviews a nationally representative sample of American adults and measures their political attitudes and activities. The advantage of these cross-sectional studies is that I can examine the preferences of a large number of respondents over a fairly long period of time. The limitation, however, is that each respondent is interviewed at only one point in time, so these data cannot tell me anything about how the opinions of individual voters may change over time. To address the question of voter change, I make use of the NES panel data studies in later analyses. The limitation of these panel data, however, is that they can examine change only over a short window of time (typically, four years). Taken together, these two types of data—cross-sectional studies and the panel data studies—will allow me to demonstrate that sorting has occurred and that elite polarization is a key cause of this increase.

Do Polarized Elites Generate Clearer Party Cues?

The first step in testing my sorting theory is to verify that more polarized elites generate clearer cues about where the parties stand on the issues. I measure voters' assessment of the parties' positions using the NES party placement items. During the course of their interview, NES respondents are asked to place both the Democratic and the Republican Party on a series of issue scales. I code a respondent as correctly identifying the parties' locations on a given issue if he places the Democrats to the left of the Republicans (i.e., if he places the Democrats at a more liberal position than the Republicans). A voter who places the parties in this order understands that Democrats are the party of the left and Republicans are the party of the right (Hetherington 2001).

One particularly attractive feature of this operationalization is that it captures the theoretical concept of interest (do you understand where the parties stand on the issues?) without placing undue burden on voters. The information shortfalls of the electorate pose no problems for this measure—this type of information can be easily discerned from campaign commercials, media reports, or conversations with well-informed friends and neighbors (see the discussion in chapter 2 on the mechanisms through which voters learn about elite positions). It should therefore not only validly capture the phenomenon of interest but also suggest how many voters— and not simply the most informed—are sorted.[2]

This measure has two notable limitations, however. First, and most importantly, my measure tests only part of my theoretical argument. Elite polarization clarifies party positions by both driving the parties apart and making them more internally homogeneous (see chapter 2). But my measure here really only captures the ideological divergence between the parties; it does not assess voters' beliefs about within-party homogeneity. Sadly, there are no over-time data on party homogeneity, so there is no way to test this portion of my argument. That said, however, I can still test the main thrust of my theoretical argument: that when voters recognize that the parties take distinct positions, they should be more likely to sort.

Second, one might object to the use of data based on respondent perceptions, arguing that I am confounding my measure of party positions

with general political knowledge (since those who know more about politics are better able to spatially order the parties; see Delli-Carpini and
Keeter 1996). While undoubtedly my measure is related to general political knowledge, the two are, in fact, distinct. The key difference between my
measure and a measure of general political knowledge is that my measure
has a particular theoretical linkage to sorting. So if I find a link between the
recognition of elite party differences and sorting, it is not simply that some
omnibus "political knowledge" explains sorting but that a particular kind
of information—information about the parties' positions on the issues—
explains sorting. In the next chapter, I compare the predictive power of
these two measures with one another, so I refer the interested reader
there for more details. But for now, I simply note that it is incorrect to
equate my measure of recognition of elite party differences developed
above with general political knowledge.[3]

I calculate my measure of awareness of party differences for the six
items asked repeatedly over time by the NES: the liberal-conservative
scale, the guaranteed jobs and a standard of living scale, the government
services and spending scale, the government (vs. private) health insurance
scale, the defense spending scale, and the aid to minorities scale. I expect
to find that more voters think the parties take clearer positions as the
parties move to the ideological poles; that is, I expect to find increasing
awareness of party differences over time. Figure 3.1 gives the trend over
time for each issue.[4]

All these measures are increasing over time, supporting the general
notion that the party positions are clearer today than they were a generation ago. This confirms Hetherington's 2001 findings about the liberal-
conservative ideological scale and demonstrates that the same arguments
also apply to a broader set of issues. As the elites have polarized, ordinary
voters increasingly understand the relative ideological positions of the
major parties.[5] These results handsomely confirm the first part of my argument: that when elites pull apart ideologically, voters will be better able to
discern where the parties stand relative to one another.[6]

But note that the trend line is not a straight shot up over time, unlike the
measures of elite polarization discussed in other works (see, e.g., McCarty,
Poole, and Rosenthal 2006). While some items—the liberal-conservative
scale, the guaranteed jobs scale—show a relatively steady climb over the
years, some of the other issue scales have different patterns, reflecting the
politics of each issue. So, for example, take the defense spending item.
The item peaks in the 1980s during the Reagan defense buildup but then

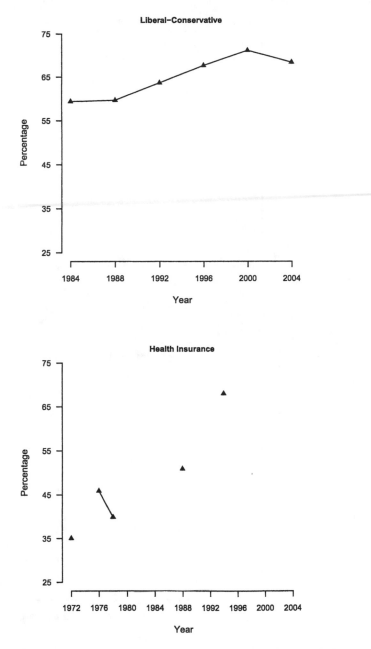

FIGURE 3.1. The percentage of respondents who can correctly place the Democratic Party to the left of the Republican Party on six issue position scales over time.

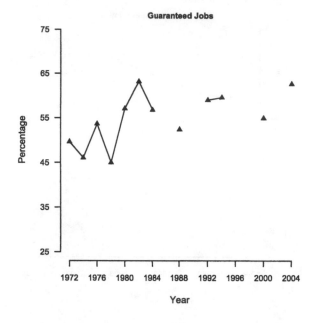

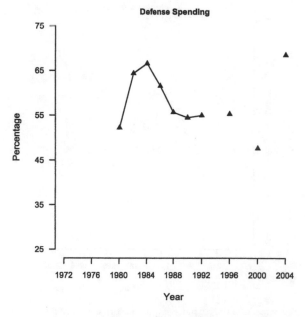

FIGURE 3.1. (*continued*)

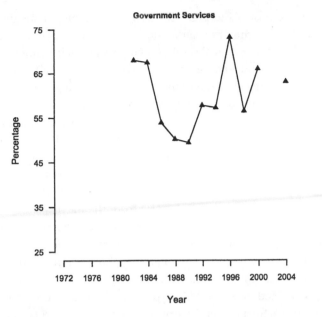

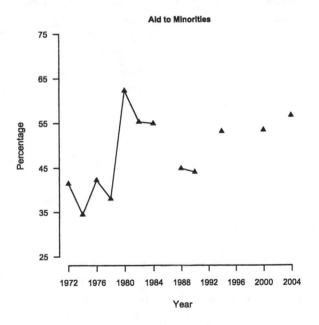

FIGURE 3.1. (*continued*)

falls off in the post–Cold War period (before jumping up again in 2004). Likewise, the government health insurance item reaches its zenith in 1994, just after the debate over the Clinton health care plan. Others—like the aid to minorities and government services scales—fall off in the late 1980s but rise again in the 1990s and 2000s. This variation highlights a subtle but important point to understanding the dynamics of mass-elite interactions. One might assume that, as elite polarization increases, a greater propor- tion of the public will automatically be able to correctly place the parties. But this is incorrect for two reasons. First, ordinary citizens do not watch NOMINATE scores and notice when there is an increase in polarization. Instead, as I discussed in the previous chapter, they listen to campaign messages, they hear (and see) rhetoric from the parties comparing their relative issue positions, they talk to well-informed friends and neighbors, they observe interest groups, and they gather information as they go about their everyday lives. They know something about where the parties stand, but that information is not particularly nuanced. So they need to see re- peated, sustained debate—like those over the Clinton health care pro- posal or Bush's Social Security privatization plan—to grasp the changes in party positions. The mass public will update its beliefs, but only in the face of clear, sustained elite shifts in positions.

Further, because voters have a history with the political parties, each individual piece of political information about the parties' positions has only a limited effect. The two major parties have existed in the United State for 150 years, and their positions on many issues have endured for decades. Parties have histories, and voters do not discard decades of ex- perience because of one new piece of information. Instead, it may take a substantial shift in positions (or repetition of the message that a smaller shift has occurred) to convince voters that a party's positions really have become clearer.[7]

Have Voters Sorted?

But have these clearer cues generated more sorting? My theory predicts that, as voters are given these clearer cues (from more polarized elites), they will use them to align their own partisanship and ideological beliefs. I test this step in my theory by examining the amount of sorting on a variety of different issues. I consider a citizen to be sorted when his position is on the same side of moderate as that of his national party elites—a sorted Democrat takes a liberal position; a sorted Republican takes a conservative one.[8] While this coding rule follows in a straightforward manner from the theoretical definition in earlier chapters, there are two related decisions that do not. First, there is the treatment of partisan leaners: are they partisans or independents? I count them as partisans, given that they behave like partisans (Keith et al. 1992). Second, many NES respondents simply do not know where they stand on the issues. These individuals can be counted as unsorted, or they can be treated as missing data (since they failed to provide a position on the issue). I count them as unsorted to avoid biasing my results: respondents who do not know where they stand on the issues typically know less about politics (Zaller 1992), so treating them as missing data might potentially give me a misleading picture of the electorate by omitting the least sophisticated voters. Readers who are made uncomfortable by these choices should be reassured by the fact that neither choice affects the ultimate substantive results.

I calculate the percentage of the electorate that is sorted on seven issues: the six issues used above (the liberal-conservative self-identification scale, the guaranteed jobs scale, the government services and spending scale, the government health insurance scale, the defense spending scale, the aid to minorities scale) and the respondents' position on abortion.[9] I expect there to be evidence of increased sorting on every issue over time (e.g., a larger percentage of the electorate should be sorted on every issue at the end of the series than at the beginning). In particular, I expect to find the highest levels of sorting in the 1990s and 2000s—this is the period in which the parties took particularly polarized positions, and these shifts were broadcast to voters. Figure 3.2 gives the percentage sorted on each issue over time.[10]

Consider first the panel that depicts sorting on the liberal-conservative scale. In 1972, 28 percent of the electorate was sorted, but that figure grows considerably over the next three decades to 46 percent in 2004. If we take into account the fact that many Americans consider themselves "moderates" or cannot locate themselves on the liberal-conservative scale—and hence cannot be sorted by definition—these trends become even more impressive. Clearly, respondents are lining up their party and ideological label today in much larger numbers than a generation ago. As the parties clarify their positions, ordinary Democrats and Republicans are moving their positions into alignment with their party elites.[11] But as I expected, there is variation over time. While the general trend is up, there is only limited change in the 1970s: the parties then were still quite heterogeneous. But in the 1990s and 2000s, there is a more marked increase in sorting as the parties (particularly the Republicans) pull apart toward

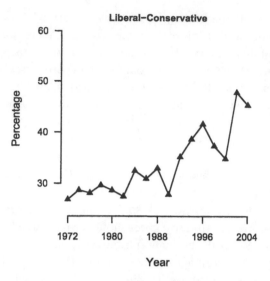

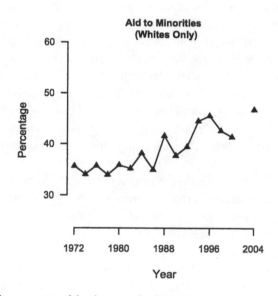

FIGURE 3.2. The percentage of the electorate that is sorted over time, broken down by issue.

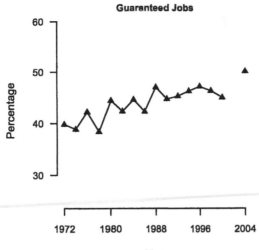

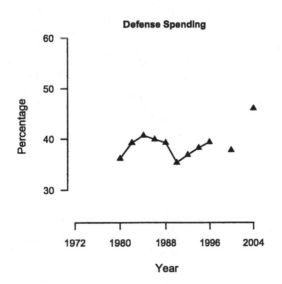

FIGURE 3.2. (*continued*)

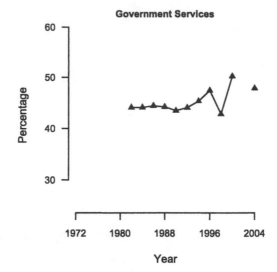

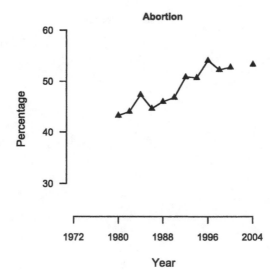

FIGURE 3.2. (*continued*)

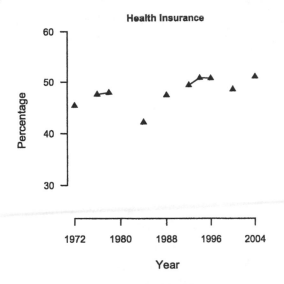

FIGURE 3.2. (*continued*)

the ideological poles (McCarty, Poole, and Rosenthal 2006).[12] The rapid increase in sorting during the 1990s and 2000s also suggests that certain major political events—like the 1994 "Republican Revolution"—play a crucial role in clarifying elites' policy positions and generating voter sorting, as the theory predicted they would in chapter 2. Overall, the pattern on liberal-conservative self-identification strongly supports my argument: as ordinary voters perceive the parties to take clearer positions, those same voters will increasingly align their party identification and their issue positions.

The patterns on the other issues also support my argument. Looking across the panels in figure 3.2, it is clear that sorting takes place to some degree on all of these issues.[13] For example, compared with 1972, 11 percent more respondents now take the same position as their partisan elites on the issue of guaranteed jobs: in 1972 only 39 percent of partisans did so; today the figure is 51 percent. Consistent with the existing literature, the mass public has become much better sorted on abortion. As Adams (1997) demonstrates, in response to elite polarization on the issue, ordinary Democrats and Republicans have increasingly pulled apart. Since 1980, an additional 10 percent of the electorate have aligned their position on abortion with the position taken by their partisan elites. Other issues, like aid to minorities, show a more sluggish pattern, with only a

7 percent increase from 1972 to 2004, though most of this increase comes in the 2000–2004 period: until 2000, the pattern was essentially flat.[14] I leave exploring these issue-specific differences for future work (see below); the main conclusion from figure 3.2 for now is that there is strong support for my sorting argument.

One might be tempted to conclude that sorting is quite limited: after all, even in 2004, only approximately 50 percent of the electorate was sorted on the liberal-conservative scale, and there was even less sorting on some issues. Given the stark levels of elite polarization, one might expect these figures to be somewhat higher, with more like 70 or 80 percent of the electorate sorted. While there may be some truth to this claim, taking it too far misses an important point about the mass public. Ordinary voters struggle to make sense of politics in any sort of abstract, ideological terms, and they struggle to achieve coherence in their political worldview (Converse 1964; Jacoby 1995; Zaller 1992; though see Ansolabehere, Rodden, and Snyder 2008 for an alternative perspective). The increases in sorting depicted in figure 3.2 represent a significant change, in both statistical and substantive terms. The amount of sorting has been considerable, and as I discuss in later chapters, has had a sizable impact on elections and governance.

The Variance in Sorting across Issues

Some readers may be puzzled by the cross-issue variation in sorting: why do some issues have much more sorting than others? Answering this question is beyond the scope of the present project, but below I spell out a number of potential hypotheses that may explain these differences.

First, and most significantly, elite positions are simply much clearer on some issues than on others. On some issues—like tax cuts or abortion—elites' cues are very clear and straightforward: almost all Democrats/Republicans take similar positions on the issue, and there are large policy differences separating the parties. On these sorts of issues the mass public tends to be reasonably well sorted. Take, as an example, President Bush's plan to add personal accounts to Social Security. This was a classic example of an issue where the elite parties were highly unified and there were stark differences between their positions. Given this, I would expect there to be fairly high levels of sorting in the mass public on this issue, and there was: in February 2005, 76 percent of the mass public was sorted on Bush's Social Security privatization plan.[15] Distinct party cues generate high levels of mass sorting, all else equal.

But on other issues, elite Democrats and Republicans take positions that are more similar to one another. Trade and immigration are two recent salient issues that divide the parties internally. On these issues, given the ambiguity of the elite cues, I would expect to see less sorting among members of the mass public—if an ordinary Democrat looks to his party elites for a position on trade, does he look to the free-trade wing or the protectionist wing? It is hard to say. Likewise, one could tell a similar story—particularly for Republicans—on the question of how to address immigration. The mass public shows a lack of sorting in response to these ambiguous elite cues. In 2007 polling data from the *Los Angeles Times*, there were few differences between partisans over their attitudes toward the value of immigrants to the American economy, their attitudes toward employers who knowingly hire illegal immigrants, or the best solution to the immigration issue (increase border security but offer a guest-worker program).[16] Given the overlap between the parties and the dissension within the Republican Party, this lack of difference between the mass parties is not particularly surprising. Overall, when the parties divide internally, take similar positions to one another, or both, we should not expect to see much mass sorting (see also Sanbonmatsu 2002; Gabel and Scheve 2007).

A second factor that might explain the lack of sorting on a given issue is the relative salience of that dimension. At some points in time, some issues simply are not discussed much by the parties, and as a result, voters have fewer opportunities to follow elite cues. At other times, when the issues are more salient, party positions become more readily accessible to voters. Take, for example, the issue of defense spending. There is little change in sorting on this issue until 2004, when there is a sharp jump upward. This likely reflects the rise in salience following the Iraq and Afghanistan conflicts, which makes the parties' relative positions on defense more prominent. But when this or other issues are less relevant, the elite cues will not be as accessible to ordinary voters (simply reflecting the fact that elites spend less time discussing these issues). So an issue's salience (or lack thereof) may also affect the percentage of the population that is sorted on that issue.

Third, valence arguments also sometimes dominate a party's message on a given issue or set of issues. The parties sometimes frame issues using valence arguments about "real security" or "effective health care," fairly vague terms that imply little policy content. When the parties frame issues this way, average Americans are hard-pressed to understand how to connect partisanship and issue positions. So on issues where these sorts of valence frames dominate, there may be less sorting.

Finally, this cross-issue variation may stem from changes in the meanings of some of the survey items. Take the issue of government aid to minorities. Issues of poverty are increasingly framed as issues of race in America, fusing the two issues together in the minds of ordinary Americans. As a result, ordinary respondents may, over time, come to equate aid to minorities with unpopular welfare programs (Gilens 1999; Kellstedt 2003). If correct, this phenomenon would decrease sorting among Democrats and increase sorting among Republicans. This is the pattern we observe in the over-time data: Republicans have become better sorted on this issue over time, while Democrats have not (see Fiorina and Levendusky 2006b). Given that this item is asked in only this one format (with only minor variations over time), I cannot convincingly conclude that this explanation actually is correct, even if the evidence seems consistent with this account. But more generally, given changing political circumstances, the meanings of questions evolve over time, which may also impact why some issues show so little sorting over time.

With a limited number of issues asked over time, it simply is not possible to subject these sorts of explanations to rigorous testing. And obviously, there may be even more prosaic reasons why some items show less sorting over time than others (e.g., difficulties in comprehension or interpretation). But overall, these factors—particularly about the degree of elite polarization, the relative salience of the issues, and the degree of valence competition—suggest reasons why sorting varies across issues. This suggests fruitful paths for future work to explore this sort of cross-sectional and intertemporal variation.

Does Sorting Vary by Demographics?

The evidence presented above makes a compelling case that sorting is the product of elite changes that allow ordinary voters to understand how party and ideology fit together. But so far, all of my evidence comes from the electorate as a whole. There may be variation in sorting among different social groups within the electorate that is missed by examining only the nation as a whole. I now explore sorting broken down by a series of demographic variables to determine the extent to which sorting is truly a national change.

Sorting in the North and the South

Perhaps the most obvious place where I would expect sorting to differ is in the South. As the South moved from conservative and Democratic to conservative and Republican, it moved from largely unsorted to largely sorted. As a result, much of the sorting I noted above may simply be a reflection of this southern realignment: sorting may be a regional, rather than a national, phenomenon. To examine this possibility, I computed the percentage of the electorate that is sorted on eight issues in both the South and the non South, where the South is defined to be the eleven states of the former Confederacy. These issues are the seven issues used earlier, plus the respondent's position on affirmative action. Figure 3.3 gives the patterns over time.

Sorting on these issues is *not* simply limited to one region but rather has occurred throughout the nation—the story of sorting is not simply the story of the southern realignment. With the exception of racial issues, there are only minor differences between northerners and southerners in terms of sorting, and the two regions move in parallel to one another. This is a story of national change rather than simply a regional one.

Racial issues are the only exception to this general pattern. For both the aid to minorities item and the more recent affirmative action item, much of the sorting has been concentrated in the South. For example, while there was only a 7 percent increase in sorting in the North on the aid to minorities item, there was a 26 percent increase in the South. The change in the South reflects the shift from the Democratic to the Republican Party in the South, so racially conservative Southerners went from out of step with the Democratic Party to more in step with the Republican Party. Here, the distinctive politics of the South do play a more important role in explaining sorting.

But simply comparing the rates of sorting misses an even more important question: which region was the more important driver of sorting? Does sorting reflect a process of "southernization," whereby the rest of the nation becomes more like the South? Or is instead sorting a process of nationalization, with the North leading the change and the South lagging behind (for a review of these arguments, see Cowden 2001)? The classic story of the evolution of the mass public suggests that southernization was at work: the change in the mass electorate was sparked by the emergence of race as a national, rather than simply a regional, issue (Carmines and Stimson 1989). More recent theories, however, suggest a process of

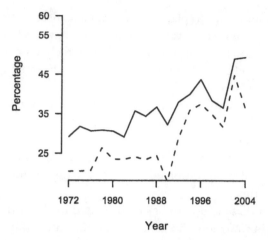

Liberal–Conservative

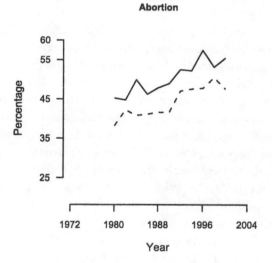

Abortion

FIGURE 3.3. The percentage of respondents who agree with their party over time on eight NES items, broken down by whether or not the respondent lives in the South. The solid lines depict sorting in the North; the dashed lines depict sorting in the South.

Guaranteed Jobs

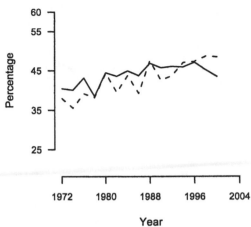

Defense Spending

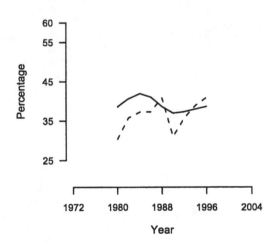

FIGURE 3.3. (*continued*)

Government Services

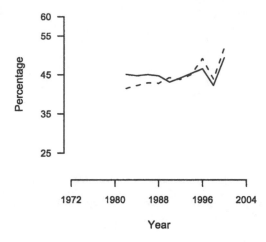

Aid to Minorities (Whites Only)

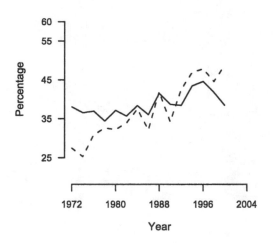

FIGURE 3.3. (*continued*)

Health Insurance

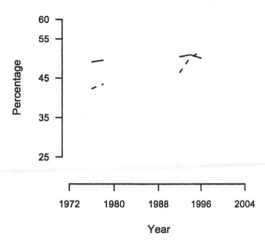

Affirmative Action (Whites Only)

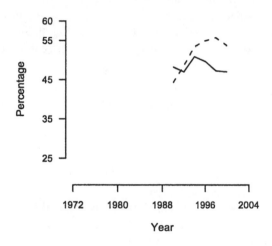

FIGURE 3.3. (*continued*)

nationalization, whereby economic development in the South generated the contemporary political alignment (Shafer and Johnston 2006; Polsby 2003).

To distinguish between these mechanisms, I examine sorting in two hypothetical scenarios. First, imagine sorting had occurred only in the South. That is, imagine that sorting had stopped in the North in 1972, and any subsequent sorting was isolated to southern respondents. Second, imagine that sorting had occurred only in the North (i.e., sorting in the South stopped in 1972). These counterfactual scenarios allow me to envision a world where sorting is the product of only one region (either the North or the South). I then ask how much smaller (or larger) sorting would be in these counterfactual scenarios. These counterfactual scenarios will allow me to assess which region was more important to the overall growth of sorting on each issue. If the South has been more important—that is, more of the increase in sorting is due to the southern change—then this supports the southernization hypothesis. On the other hand, if sorting is primarily the result of changes outside the South, then this suggests that a process of nationalization—not Southernization—drives sorting.

Figure 3.4 depicts these counterfactual scenarios. Begin with the first panel. The solid line shows how sorting on the liberal-conservative self-identification scale would change without the North. Numbers larger than 0 indicate that sorting would be *higher* without the North, numbers smaller than 0 indicate that sorting would be lower without the North. Here, we see that, over time, sorting would be lower—quite a bit lower—without the North. For example, in 2004, sorting on the liberal-conservative scale would be 14 percent lower without the North. In contrast, without the South, sorting on this item would be only 5 percent lower. In every year, changes in the North are changing the national dynamics of sorting, at least on the liberal-conservative scale. This supports the nationalization hypothesis: it is sorting in the North, rather than the South, that is the primary driver of sorting on the liberal-conservative scale.

The other panels in figure 3.4 show support for both patterns over time. Some issues support a nationalization hypothesis (guaranteed jobs, abortion), while other suggest southernization was at work (racial issues, the government services and spending trade-off, and the health care item). The most striking pattern, however, is that, with the exception of the aid to minorities item, these differences are quite small (typically less than 10 percent). The overall pattern across issues suggests that both southernization and nationalization drive sorting at different times and on

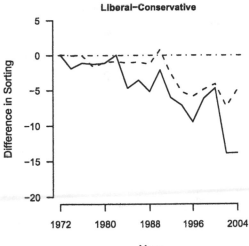

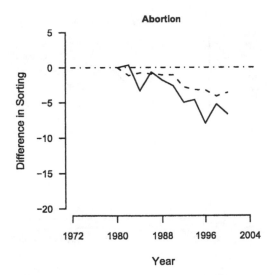

FIGURE 3.4. The difference between observed sorting and sorting under two counterfactual scenarios. The solid line shows the difference between actual sorting and the amount of sorting if sorting in the North had stopped in 1972. The dashed line shows the difference between actual sorting and the amount of sorting if sorting had stopped in the South in 1972.

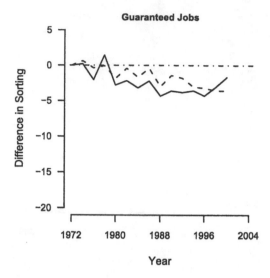

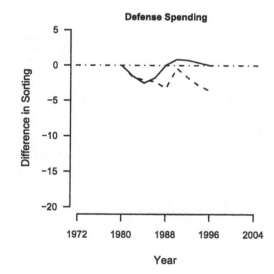

FIGURE 3.4. (*continued*)

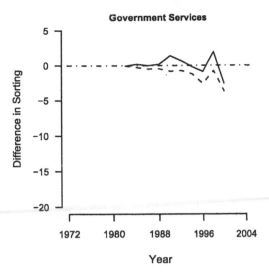

Government Services

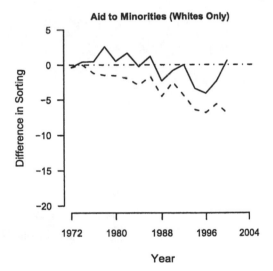

Aid to Minorities (Whites Only)

FIGURE 3.4. (*continued*)

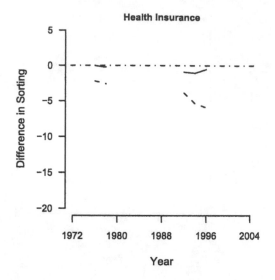

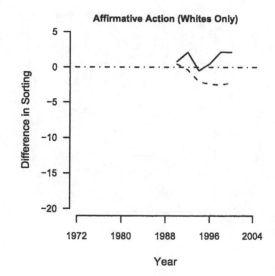

FIGURE 3.4. (*continued*)

different issues; future work will be needed to tease apart why these patterns differ across time and issues. The important conclusion for the current discussion, however, is that both processes appear to be at work, which implies that both regions—not just one—are crucial to the story of sorting.

But there is a vital caveat to this conclusion. Even when the data are consistent with a nationalization hypothesis, the South still played a crucial role in the sorting process because of the key role of southern elites. It was movements by conservative Democratic elites from the South that initially generated the process of elite polarization that precipitated sorting throughout the nation (Perlstein 2001; McCarty, Poole, and Rosenthal 2006). Similarly, how the parties reacted to the question of civil rights in the South helped to shape their destinies for the next generation, not only in the South but throughout the nation (Kruse 2005; Crespino 2007). It is something of an irony that the North and the South can look similar today (in terms of sorting) because the South was so distinctive forty years ago. So clearly, the South—and its unique legacy of race—matter to the transformation of the American electorate. But my results here also imply that changes outside the South are equally important.

Sorting by Birth Cohort

The increase in sorting may also be a function of cohort replacement: sorting increases because younger, better-sorted voters enter the electorate and replace older, less well sorted voters. These cohort effects stem from theories of political socialization, which argue that the strength of the relationship between party and ideology is largely shaped by the individual's political environment when they come of age politically. Afterward, their attitudes and partisanship crystallize enough to resist environmental factors like elite polarization (Stoker and Jennings 2008). Older voters, who came of age during an era of factionalized parties (Han and Brady 2007), will be less likely to be sorted than younger voters, who came of age during an era of intense elite partisanship.

I decompose sorting by birth cohort for four issues asked repeatedly over time: the liberal-conservative scale, the guaranteed jobs scale, the aid to minorities scale, and the abortion scale (other issues show similar patterns; I use only four issues here in the interest of simplicity). While generational replacement should explain at least part of the sorting on every issue, there should also be systematic differences between issues rooted in each issue's unique political development. For the liberal-conservative self-identification scale, I would expect to find that replacement dominates conversion as the explanation for sorting. Many of the most dramatic elite-level changes have occurred over the past ten to fifteen years, and by that point, many older voters will have more crystallized beliefs and hence resist change. It should be younger voters entering the electorate who are driving much of this change.

Given that the parties have been polarized on New Deal issues such as government job guarantees for more than half a century, I expect even the oldest cohorts to be reasonably well sorted on this issue. At the same time, the parties have remained divided on the issue, and as a result, younger cohorts should be better sorted, though the differences between cohorts should be relatively small. On this issue, then, it should be a case of sorting driven by both within- and between-cohort change.

Generational replacement should almost completely explain sorting on abortion. The parties did not take distinct and coherent positions on abortion until the early 1980s (Adams 1997), so the oldest cohorts should display little evidence of sorting. For these voters, abortion became politicized after they had formed their worldviews, so abortion needed to be grafted onto an existing political outlook. For younger voters, by contrast, abortion was more organically part of their political orientation, so abortion attitudes should be more strongly related to partisanship (Stoker and Jennings 2008). Additionally, given that abortion is the sort of emotional "easy" issue on which citizens tend to have reasonably stable views (Carmines and Stimson 1980), there should be somewhat less conversion evident on this sort of issue.

I expect that the pattern for the aid to minorities item will parallel the one for abortion: sorting here too should be primarily the product of generational replacement rather than within-cohort conversion (Carmines and Stimson 1989). Given that the parties divided on this issue beginning in the 1960s, however, there should be earlier evidence of sorting on this issue. Figure 3.5 gives the amount of sorting on each of these four issues broken down by cohort over time.[17]

Generational replacement plays a role in sorting for all four issues. In recent years, older voters are typically 7–8 percent less well sorted on the liberal-conservative scale, and 3–4 percent less well sorted on the aid to minorities item. Generational replacement clearly explains at least some of the aggregate increase in sorting over time.

Abortion demonstrates the clearest and largest between-cohort difference over time: in 2004, the younger cohort was approximately 7 percent

Liberal–Conservative

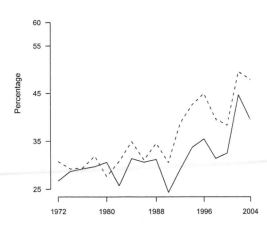

Abortion

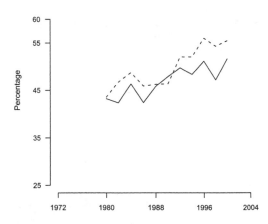

FIGURE 3.5. The percentage of respondents who are sorted on four issues over time, broken down by cohort. The solid lines represent those born between 1911 and 1942, and the dashed lines represent those born between 1943 and 1974.

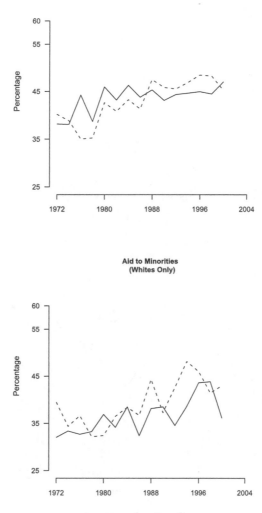

FIGURE 3.5. (*continued*)

better sorted than the older cohort. While both cohorts have become better sorted over time (suggesting there is some within-cohort conversion
even here), cohort replacement is a significant part of the story. This is
what one would expect: abortion emerged on the stage when the older
voters were approaching middle age, so for them, their stand on abortion
has always been a less coherent part of their political identity than for
younger voters.

But perhaps more surprisingly, with the exception of abortion, it is within-cohort change—not between-cohort replacement—that is the primary driver of sorting. Take, for example, the government's role to guarantee each citizen a job. Although the younger cohort is consistently better sorted, both cohorts show approximately a 9–10 percent increase in sorting between 1972 and 2004. On the liberal-conservative scale, the older cohort changes rapidly in the 1990s as the parties pull apart ideologically, moving from 24 percent sorted in 1990 to 39 percent sorted in 2004. Likewise, even on the question of racial issues—where one would expect attitudes to be quite resistant to change—the older cohort moves from 34 percent sorted to 47 percent sorted, a 13 percent increase over the past thirty years. On these issues, while generational replacement is important, within-cohort change is arguably the dominant factor.

Although within-cohort change is the dominant factor driving sorting on most issues, patterns of cohort replacement have an important implication for the long-term levels of sorting in the electorate. Today's elite-level patterns shape sorting not only for today but for years to come. While many voters clearly respond to contemporaneous elite changes (e.g., even some older voters sort in response to elite polarization), the attitudes of others are set in early adulthood and undergo only minor changes thereafter. So even if elites suddenly became less polarized today, sorting will still persist due to these socialization effects. I return to this point in the concluding chapter, where it will have implications for the long-term patterns of sorting in the electorate.

The Rise of Evangelical Christians and Sorting on Abortion

The previous two demographic changes—the southern realignment and generational replacement—explain the rise of sorting across a wide host of issues. But there is another fundamental demographic shift that has affected sorting, albeit primarily on one set of issues: the rise of evangelical Christians and the politics of social issues, especially abortion. The past few decades have seen a fundamental shift in the religious composition of the Republican Party, with evangelical Protestants replacing mainline Protestants. During this same time frame, the Republican Party has also pulled sharply to the right on abortion (Layman 2001). This raises an interesting puzzle: to what extent is the mass Republican Party's opposition to abortion rights driven by the shift in party composition from mainline to evangelical Christians, and to what extent is it driven by other segments of the party becoming more pro-life over time?

I use the abortion index in the General Social Survey (GSS) to answer this question. The GSS is another high-quality, nationally representative academic survey similar to the NES. The major difference between them is that the GSS focuses primarily on social issues rather than political ones. The GSS therefore provides a richer battery of items related to social issues, including abortion and religion, than does the NES.[18]

The GSS measures abortion attitudes by asking respondents whether or not they would allow abortion in six circumstances: if the pregnancy endangers the life or health of the mother; if the pregnancy is the result of rape; if there is a significant risk of serious birth defects; if the woman is poor and cannot afford another child; if she is married and does not want any more children; and if she is not married and does not want to marry the father. Using these items, I calculate the permissiveness of abortion attitudes (e.g., the number of scenarios where the respondent would allow legal abortion) for evangelical and nonevangelical Republicans as well as Democrats. If the sorting on abortion reflects primarily the entry of conservative evangelical Christians into the Republican Party, then nonevangelical Republicans should not change their level of support for abortion over time. Rather, the growing support for abortion restrictions in the Republican Party should reflect the larger numbers of evangelical and fundamentalist Christians in the Republican coalition. If, by contrast, all Republicans, regardless of religious faith, are becoming better sorted over time, then both evangelical and nonevangelical Republicans alike should display less support for abortion rights over time. Figure 3.6 gives the patterns from 1972 to 2004.[19]

Fundamentalist/evangelical Republicans are always the most strongly opposed to abortion rights, which should come as no surprise given their doctrinal beliefs. The increasing proportion of evangelicals and other fundamentalist Christians in the Republican Party clearly explains a considerable amount of the growth in opposition to abortion rights among Republicans. But note too that even nonevangelical Republicans have become less supportive of abortion rights since 1990. This pattern of results suggests that all Republicans, regardless of religious persuasion, are responding to the pro-life rhetoric of elites.[20] The growing number of evangelical Protestants in the Republican Party explains a considerable amount, but not all, of the party sorting on abortion. All Republicans—regardless of whether or not they are evangelicals—have become less supportive of abortion rights over time (both by driving away Republicans who support abortion rights and by converting other Republicans to a

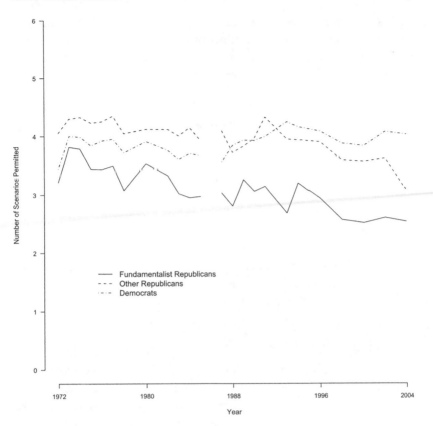

FIGURE 3.6. The average number of circumstances (out of six) in which the respondents would permit legal abortion, broken down by party and religious fundamentalism.

more pro-life position). I do not want to push this argument too far: the party's rhetoric is conditional on its supporters, so with fewer evangelicals, perhaps Republican elites would have discussed abortion less frequently, leading to less party differentiation (especially among nonevangelicals) on this issue. But overall, sorting on abortion appears to be driven not just by the rise of evangelicals within the Republican Party but also by cue taking from partisan elites more broadly.

Looking across all three demographic factors—region, birth cohort, and religious fundamentalism—the same basic pattern emerges. Yes, there are key differences based on the history of an issue or a region. But regardless of these differences, the basic story of elites clarifying their po-

sitions and voters responding by sorting emerges as well. Understanding
these subgroup differences and their origins is clearly a vital part of the
sorting story. But the dominant cause of sorting remains the elite polarization mechanism discussed in earlier chapters.

Considerable Sorting, Limited Polarization

In chapter 1, I argued that while elite polarization generates considerable
mass sorting, it does not generate much additional mass polarization. The
analysis above demonstrates that the first part of this claim is correct: as
elites become more polarized, ordinary voters become better sorted. But
I now need to provide the evidence for the second part of that claim: that
this sorting generates only a very modest increase in mass polarization. I
do this in two steps. First, I demonstrate that there has been only a small
increase in mass polarization over the past few decades, and then I show
that sorting itself is the cause of this increase in polarization.

A More Polarized America?

As I discussed in chapter 1, scholars remain divided over the extent of polarization in the mass public. The proponents of a more polarized American public argue that ordinary citizens have become more likely to take
extreme positions and less likely to take moderates ones. They argue that
Americans have moved away from the center and toward the extremes
over time (see Abramowitz 2006, especially his fig. 2-10 and table 2-3).
Note that the claim is *not* simply that partisan polarization (e.g., sorting)
has increased. Rather, these authors claim that ordinary Americans are
more ideologically extreme, and less centrist, overall—they argue that
mass polarization has increased. They conclude that "American politics
are highly polarized—and that is true not just for political leaders and
party elites, but for the public and the electorate as well. The public has
been significantly polarized for some time and in recent years has become
more so" (Campbell 2006b, 153). It is not merely political elites who are
polarized, but the mass public is as well.[21]

Yet these claims have been fiercely contested. Examining over-time
data, these authors conclude that American views have become more similar, not less (DiMaggio, Evans, and Bryson 1996; Evans 2003). The most
prominent work on this topic—Fiorina, Abrams, and Pope's 2005 *Culture*

War?— finds that ordinary Americans are centrist and moderate, with little evidence of electoral polarization. A host of analyses by other scholars, from a variety of different methodological approaches, reach similar conclusions (Baker 2005; McCarty, Poole, and Rosenthal 2006; Wolfe 1999). There may be a variety of important divisions between ordinary Americans, but they remain relatively centrist and moderate.

But which perspective is correct? The answer is ambiguous, and I turn to the NES data to resolve this impasse. If ordinary Americans have become more polarized over time, two trends should be visible in the data (see the theoretical discussion in chapter 1). First, voters should be less moderate and more extreme over time, and second, there should be evidence of increasing bimodality in the distribution of public opinion. To assess the evidence for these expectations, I use the NES data to construct an over-time measure of respondents' preferences. In particular, I turn to six items asked in every quadrennial presidential election-year survey since 1984: the guaranteed jobs scale, the government services and spending scale, the defense spending scale, the government health insurance scale, the aid to minorities scale, and the abortion scale.

To assess the amount of polarization, I compare the distribution of responses in 1984 to the distribution in 2004. My focus is on shifts in the distribution of ideology: has there been movement away from the center and toward the extremes? Figure 3.7 gives kernel density plots (smoothed histograms) of respondents' average positions across these six items in both 1984 and 2004.[22] There is some evidence of polarization: there are fewer moderates in 2004 than in 1984. At the same time, these data are hardly bimodal: the area at the extremes has not particularly increased— if anything, it has decreased slightly. Comparing the two density plots, it appears that some respondents who used to sit in the center of the ideological distribution are now just to one side or the other: respondents who were previously moderate have now chosen a side. But at the same time, the majority of the electorate remain closer to the center than to the poles. Although there is clearly some increased polarization over this twenty-year window, it is also important to note that the population is still (approximately) normally distributed along a left-right ideological dimension, with far more respondents in the center of the distribution than on the extremes. The electorate (at least using these measures) remains more moderate than extreme.

To examine these changes in more detail, I grouped the data into four categories based on the degree of ideological extremity. I want to examine

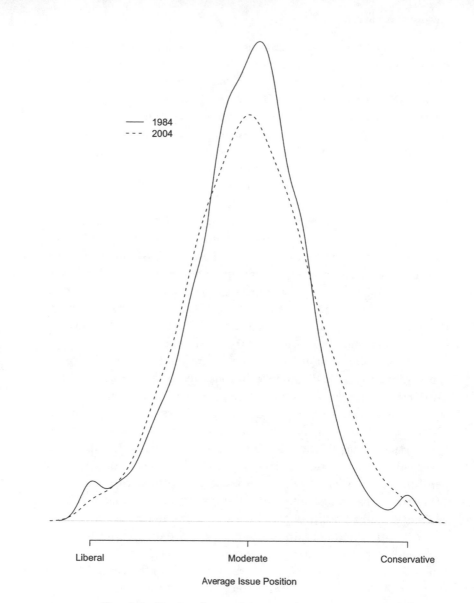

FIGURE 3.7. Kernel density plot of respondents' average position across six policy items common to both the 1984 and 2004 NES.

TABLE 3.1 **Changes in degree of ideological extremity between 1984 and 2004**

Category	1984	2004	Change
Most extreme	3.7	3.1	−0.6
	11.2	16.8	5.6
	45.8	46.4	0.6
Most moderate	39.3	33.6	−5.7

Note: All cell entries are percentages. The column labeled "Change" gives the change from 1984 to 2004. Positive numbers in this column indicate categories where there were more respondents in 2004 than in 1984; negative entries, the reverse.

which groups grow larger and which grow smaller over time. Does the number of extremists grow? What about the number of centrists? Those between the center and the extremes? Table 3.1 gives the breakdown of the data from figure 3.7. Consistent with the discussion above, these data do show some evidence of increased polarization: the sharpest decline has come from the most moderate respondents. However, the extremes have hardly changed at all, with less than a 1 percent change in the number of extremists over time, and it is in the *wrong* direction: there were more extremists in 1984, not 2004. The groups between the center and the extremes experienced the largest growth over time. Voters have chosen a side and are therefore somewhat less centrist, but they have not become extremists.

To ensure that the aggregate analysis had not obscured any issue-specific trends, I also examined the degree of polarization on each item. To do this, I computed the percentage of respondents on each issue who took an "extreme" position (e.g., a position at the ends of the NES policy scales). Figure 3.8 gives the relevant breakdowns for each issue.

For clarity, I have broken these items into two graphs: one for economic issues and one for other types of issues. The same pattern emerges for all items: there is no evidence of issue-specific polarization. The only possible exception is the aid to minorities item, where there is an overall increase in the number of respondents taking the most conservative position ("blacks should help themselves"). While abortion attitudes show a much greater percentage of respondents on the extremes, respondents have become *less* extreme since 1992. The fact that abortion generates so many extreme respondents probably has as much to do with the number of response options (four response options as opposed to seven response options for the other items) as it does with the passion abortion engenders among many Americans. These issue-specific trends reinforce the pooled analysis

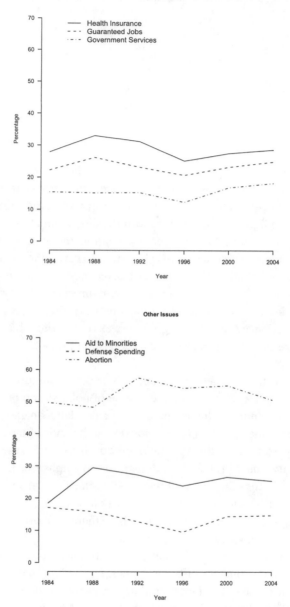

FIGURE 3.8. Percentage of respondents taking extreme positions on each of six salient issues in the NES, 1984–2004.

conducted earlier. While American have become less centrist over time, they have not become extremists. Most Americans remain closer to the center of the ideological distribution than to the extremes (see also Fiorina and Levendusky 2006a).

Does Sorting Increase Polarization?

The evidence above suggests that there has been a modest increase in polarization over time. But what drives this increase? One potential answer is sorting itself: as voters choose a side of the political aisle, they move away from the center and toward the ideological extremes, thereby increasing polarization. To test this hypothesis, I turn to the NES panel data studies—particularly the 1992-1994-1996 panel study—to examine how sorting affects ideological extremity. The panel data are ideally suited to this task: they allow me to examine how voters change over time, so I can determine whether or not voter sorting generates increases in mass polarization.

If sorting can account for the increased aggregate polarization observed above, I should observe respondents moving away from the center and toward their same-party elites when they sort. Any such shifts, however, should be quite limited in scope, because the analysis above suggests that the aggregate movements (even over a twenty-year period) are quite limited. Looking at respondents who sort between 1992 and 1996, I find that the typical movement on the seven-point liberal-conservative scale due to sorting is quite small. The median amount of change is 1 unit (on the seven-point scale), and the mean amount of change is between 1.5 and 2 units. This suggests that most people are not moving from "very liberal" to "very conservative" but rather from "moderate" to "slightly liberal" or "slightly liberal" to "slightly conservative." Sorting makes voters less centrist, but does not make them extremists.

It could also be the case that there are delayed effects of sorting on polarization: while the immediate effect of sorting on mass polarization is quite modest, there may be an effect in later periods. I test this hypothesis with data on respondents who were unsorted in 1992 but sorted in 1994. If this hypothesis is correct, then I expect to find that these individuals are more ideologically extreme in 1996 than they were in 1994.

The data, however, fail to support this hypothesis. On average, there is only a minor amount of attitude polarization after sorting (the median amount of change is 1 unit). Sorting may cause respondents to become slightly more extreme, but it does not cause voters to move all the way to the ideological poles. And it appears that the process of increasing extremity does not continue over time. Respondents who were sorted in 1992, 1994, and 1996 did not change their ideological identification at all (the median amount of change is 0 units) between 1994 and 1996. While sorting does shift respondents toward the ideological poles, the process stops far short of complete polarization.

The limitation of this analysis is, of course, that I have panel data only over a short window of time: no more than four years. My conclusions are therefore necessarily limited: I cannot examine, for example, how an individual voter shifts over longer periods of time (like several decades). As a result, I can accurately claim only that my results are consistent with the hypothesis that sorting is the factor driving the increase in mass polarization. That said, the consistency of these findings—plus results reported elsewhere (Levendusky, forthcoming)—strongly suggests that this is the correct mechanism.

Sorting is at least partially responsible for the observed increase in mass polarization. When respondents sort, they move away from the center and toward the ideological poles, thereby increasing polarization. But the extent of that movement is quite limited and results in only a small increase in mass polarization, even over a span of several decades. When respondents sort, they choose a side, but they do not become ideological extremists. The aggregate distribution of ideology is therefore less centrist and somewhat more polarized as a result of sorting, but the extent of that polarization should not be exaggerated.[23]

In the final assessment of mass polarization, it is also important to recognize that even the amount of sorting is more limited than is sometimes claimed. As I discussed earlier, there are important functional limits on sorting, and on no issue does the percentage of the electorate that is sorted approach 100 percent (or even, say, 80 percent). Although the mass parties are now farther apart than in the past on a host of issues, there is still considerable overlap between them and heterogeneity within them. It is undeniable that ordinary Democrats and Republicans now take more distinct positions on a host of issues than they did years ago. Yet at the same time, they are hardly "different tribes of a still sharply divided nation" (Balz 2007). There is more commonality among ordinary voters than is commonly assumed.

But overall, this evidence provides strong support for the argument I made in chapter 1: elite polarization has generated considerable mass sorting, which in turn has slightly increased polarization in the electorate. While the distribution of ideology within each party has shifted (sorting), the aggregate distribution of ideology has changed only a small amount (polarization). In effect, this demonstrates that both claims made in the mass polarization literature are partially correct. The proponents of polarization are correct that there has been some increase in mass polarization over time, but their critics are also correct that this increase has been quite modest. The key is that the observed increase in polarization is, in fact, due to voter sorting. Voter sorting provides the key step needed to reconcile these two competing points of view.

Conclusion

The aggregate level evidence used in this chapter demonstrates compelling support for three important empirical claims. First, the electorate is much better sorted today than a generation ago. Party and ideology are more tightly aligned in the mass electorate today than they were a generation ago. Second, recognition of elite polarization appears to be a primary mechanism explaining that change. As various elites clarified what it meant to be a Democrat or a Republican throughout the 1970s, 1980s, and 1990s, more and more voters sorted. This sorting stems from both conversion and replacement. Finally, while there has been a large degree of elite polarization and voter sorting, there has been only a much more limited amount of mass polarization. Further, what mass polarization exists is primarily the product of voter sorting itself.

There is an important limitation to one of these key findings, however: the evidence above linking elite polarization and mass sorting does not consider any rival hypotheses that might explain mass sorting. To give a more persuasive account of the linkage between elite polarization and mass sorting, I need to demonstrate that this relationship survives even when controlling for other theoretically relevant factors. I turn to this task in the next chapter.

CHAPTER FOUR

Testing Competing Explanations for Sorting

The evidence in chapter 3 supports two key claims: first, elite polarization has clarified where the parties stand on the issues of the day, and second, in response to that increased clarity, ordinary voters have sorted. While this evidence is compelling, it is also incomplete—it considers only this one explanation for sorting. While I demonstrated an association between sorting and elite polarization, this relationship may not hold once I control for other relevant factors that also affect sorting. Elite polarization is most likely the primary factor driving mass sorting, but it is not the only explanation in the literature. Unfortunately, the extant literature contains very few multivariate models of sorting that test whether the elite polarization theory is still supported once the researcher controls for other relevant covariates. This chapter offers such a model.

The Competing Hypotheses

There are several competing explanations for why individuals sort. Here, I briefly review the logic of each competing account.

RECOGNITION OF ELITE PARTY DIFFERENCES   This is the hypothesis laid out in chapter 2 and evaluated at the aggregate level in chapter 3. As elites polarize, they clarify where they stand on the issues of the day. This increased clarity should make it simpler for ordinary voters to align their partisanship and issue positions (see chapter 2 for the details of this theory). But as I argued in chapter 3, this effect is conditional on respondents' recognition that the cues have become more distinct—respondents have to realize that the elites' parties now take different ideological positions. Therefore, I expect that respondents who understand that the Democratic and Republican parties take contrasting ideological positions will be more likely to sort, *ceteris paribus*.

THE CHANGING SOUTHERN DEMOCRAT   Over the period of this study, the South has undergone a fundamental change. Half a century ago, southern Democrats were more conservative than their northern counterparts, and the southern Republican Party existed only in skeletal form. But as the South gradually realigned, that difference has largely disappeared. Today, even at the mass level, southern Democrats and Republicans look similar to their northern counterparts (Black and Black 2002). So in the early years of this study, southern Democrats should be less likely to be sorted than their northern counterparts, but that difference should decrease over time.

GENERAL POLITICAL INFORMATION   The amount of general information a respondent possesses about politics and public affairs should affect their probability of being sorted. This follows from the large body of researching demonstrating that those with higher levels of factual knowledge about politics are the most likely to behave like elites (Zaller 1992; Sniderman, Brody, and Tetlock 1991; Delli-Carpini and Keeter 1996). The politically well-informed should be the most likely to understand the elite ideological and partisan alignment and mirror that alignment in their own positions. Therefore, all else equal, the higher a respondent's general level of knowledge about politics, the more likely he is to be sorted.

VARIATION BY BIRTH COHORT   A long line of political socialization research argues that citizens' political attitudes are primarily influenced by the environment in which they come of age politically (Jennings and Niemi 1981). After early adulthood, attitudes should crystallize and become more resistant to change over time. This implies that generational replacement is a key source of sorting (Stoker and Jennings 2008). I outlined this logic in the previous chapter: elites have their largest effect on young voters, whose positions are still malleable and likely to change (in contrast to older voters, whose positions will be more rigid). So the positions taken by the parties when a voter is coming of age have an effect not only at that point in time but for the voter's entire life. Sorting should therefore be highest among the set of respondents who came of age when elite polarization was fairly high. Functionally, this implies that the youngest cohorts should be the most well sorted cohorts.

OTHER DEMOGRAPHIC CONTROLS   Finally, I include several other demographic controls that might affect whether or not respondents are sorted. Here, I include controls for race (Dawson 1994), gender (Whirls 1986), and income (McCarty, Poole, and Rosenthal 2006) to help control for other known influences on respondents' choice of partisanship and ideological self-identification.

Operationalizing Key Variables

Before I can move to my actual empirical tests of these hypotheses, I need to operationalize the relevant variables. My two main variables—the dependent variable (sorting) and the recognition of elite party differences— are operationalized the same way they were in the previous chapter. A respondent is sorted if he shares his ideological self-identification with his national party elites (e.g., he is a liberal Democrat or a conservative Republican). While I focus here on sorting on the liberal-conservative self-identification scale, I obtain similar results for other issues as well (see below). For recognizing elite party differences, I rely on the placements of the national parties on the NES issue scales. As before, a respondent recognizes that the parties take distinct positions if he places the Democratic Party to the left of the Republican Party (see chapter 3 for additional details).

To test the hypothesis about the effects of general political information, I would ideally build an additive index of items tapping factual political knowledge (Luskin and Bullock 2006). However, the number of items varies each year, and it would be difficult to construct a comparable index across years. Therefore, I fall back on the indicator included in every year: the interviewer's subjective assessment of the respondent's level of political information, a commonly used measure of political knowledge (Zaller 1992; Bartels 1996).[1]

Some readers may be concerned that my measure of respondent's recognition of elite party differences is too closely related to the measure of general political information. As I discussed in chapter 3, while the two measures are obviously related, they are far from analogous. In particular, there is a specific causal mechanism underlying one's recognition of elite party differences that explains *how* this information drives voter sorting (see chapter 2). However, by including both measures in the same model, I set up a strict test of my theory. If I am wrong and these two measures are simply analogous, then the collinearity this induces in my model should make it more difficult for me to obtain a statistically significant coefficient on my theoretically relevant variable.

The other key hypotheses—the evolution of southern Democrats and variation by birth cohort—are more straightforward to operationalize. For the southern Democrat hypothesis, I define the South as the former Confederate states, and Democrats are those who identify with or lean toward the Democratic Party. The birth cohort variables are based on coding birth year into fifteen-year birth cohorts; see the appendix for more details. Likewise, the other demographic control variables (income, race, gender) all rely on the standard NES demographic items.

An Over-Time Test

To examine both the determinants of sorting and also how those factors change over time, I estimate parallel regressions in each year for which the NES has collected the necessary data (i.e., I estimated the same regression equation separately by year: once in 1992, again in 1994, etc.). I estimate the model for every year between 1972 and 2004 except for 2000 and 2002. In 2002, two important variables are missing from the survey: income (which, while not technically missing, differs from other years in key ways that would prevent its inclusion in the model) and, more importantly, the recognition of elite polarization variable. Given these limitations, I exclude 2002 from the analysis. I also exclude 2000 from the results below due to data availability: given the split-sample design of 2000 and ensuing question availability, the usable 2000 sample is approximately one-half the size of other years, and hence the ensuing standard errors are much larger. None of the results below would change if 2000 were included, but the larger standard errors would make it more difficult to see the changes over time in the other years. Figure 4.1 plots the estimated coefficients and 95% confidence intervals for the regression from each year.[2]

Several of the hypotheses above are significant predictors of sorting. In particular, the coefficient for recognition of elite polarization is positive

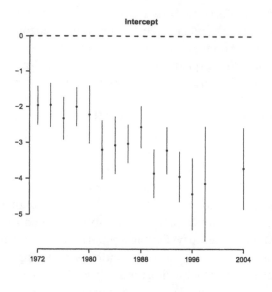

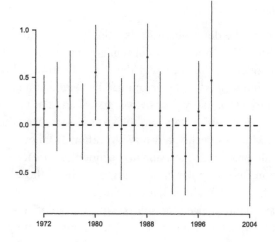

FIGURE 4.1. Graphical summary of logistic regressions predicting sorting from 1972 to 2004. Each year represents a separate regression equation. The solid dots are point estimates, and the vertical lines are 95 percent confidence intervals.

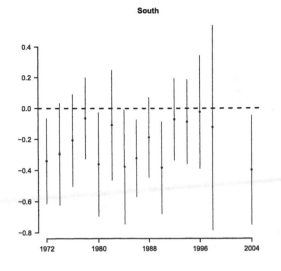

South

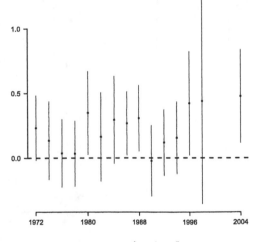

Highest Third, Income

FIGURE 4.1. (*continued*)

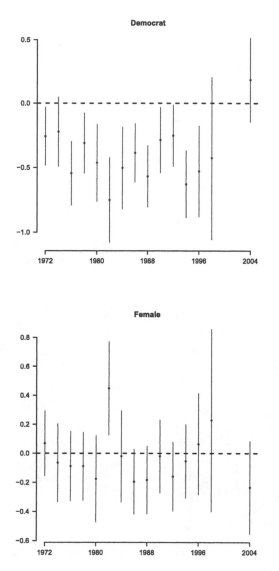

FIGURE 4.1. (*continued*)

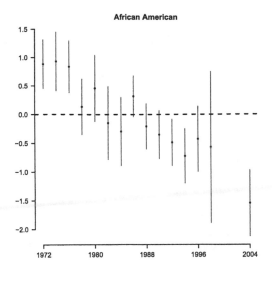

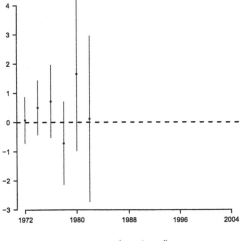

FIGURE 4.1 (*continued*)

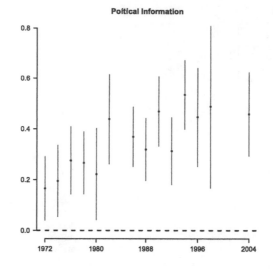

Political Information

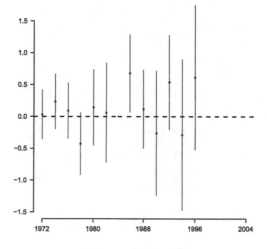

Born 1895–1910

FIGURE 4.1 *(continued)*

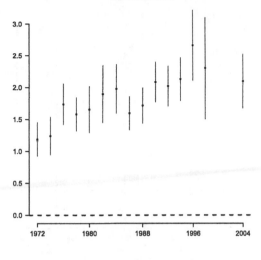

Elite Polarization

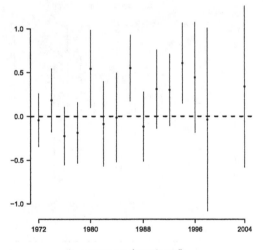

Born 1927–1942

FIGURE 4.1 *(continued)*

Born 1943–1958

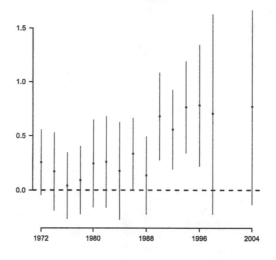

Born 1959–1974

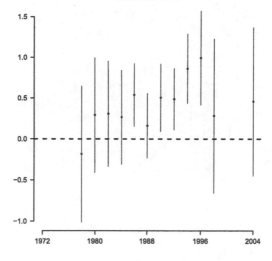

FIGURE 4.1 *(continued)*

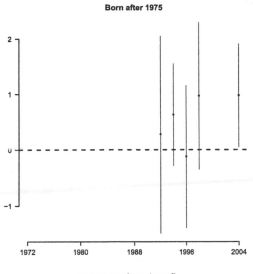

FIGURE 4.1 (*continued*)

and statistically significant in each year, even when controlling for general political information. It is incorrect to simply claim that my recognition of elite party differences variable simply captures general political knowledge. If a respondent understands how the elite parties line up ideologically, he understands how his party and ideology should be aligned.

The same pattern holds for those with higher levels of political information. We know that these voters possess more awareness about politics and public affairs and should be the most likely to mimic the elite party-ideology arrangement. And this is exactly the pattern we see in every year—as political information increases, so does the probability of being sorted.

The other demographic controls (with two exceptions) tend to have very minor effects on sorting. Gender and income are almost never statistically significant, suggesting that these variables are not important determinants of sorting after controlling for the relevant attitudinal factors. The exceptions to this pattern are cohort effects and race. While many of the cohort effects are consistently not significant, the data *do* suggest that younger voters (those born after 1943) are more likely to sort (relative to the baseline cohort, voters born between 1911 and 1926). So respondents who entered the electorate after the 1960s—when elites began to divide—are somewhat more likely to be sorted, though the effect is not particularly consistent in all years. There is a consistent pattern, however, for African Americans. They are significantly less likely to be sorted than respondents of other races, all else equal. Although African Americans are overwhelmingly Democratic and liberal on economic issues (Dawson 1994), it appears they are less likely to call themselves "liberal." This is an interesting finding I leave for future research, noting for the purposes at hand that, overall, with the exception of race and age, demographics tend to exert a weak influence on sorting.[3]

Extending These Findings

The results above suggest two important findings: first, that even controlling for other important factors, recognition of elite polarization emerges as a key explanation for mass sorting, and second, this result holds across time. But these results are limited in that they cover sorting on only one issue: the liberal-conservative self-identification scale. Does this same pattern of results hold on other issues? I have reestimated the model discussed above for every issue for which the NES asks the necessary items. The results are unambiguous: the same pattern of results emerges on every issue. This model of sorting is not limited simply to sorting on the liberal-conservative self-identification scale but extends more generally across issues.

Further, I have also used measures of actual elite polarization (measured via DW-NOMINATE; see Poole and Rosenthal 1997) in lieu of my measure of perception of elite polarization. This gives me a robustness check to ensure that my results are not dependent upon using that particular measure. Here again, the primary results replicate: elite polarization again emerges as a key determinant of mass sorting (all of these supplemental results are available in the online appendix). Overall, the findings reported in this section appear to be quite robust, and there is substantial evidence of a linkage between recognition of elite party differences and mass sorting across a variety of different items, measures, and time periods.

Establishing the Direction of the Relationship

The results in the previous section are compelling, but they are limited in an important way. Because I have only cross-sectional data, I cannot definitively rule out the possibility that I have reversed the causal logic in the story above: it could be the case that respondents first become sorted and *then* understand that Democrats are to the left of Republicans. While I think this possibility is theoretically specious, it cannot be discarded based on a cross-sectional regression. In order to determine the direction of the relationship, I need to use another set of data and statistical techniques.

How can I determine whether recognition of elite party differences leads to sorting or the reverse? The NES panel data allow me to resolve this quandary because I can use them to examine *how* respondents change over time: do they first change their beliefs about elites and then sort, or the reverse? After analyzing the panel data, I will have a more dynamic picture of respondent attitudes and behavior, and as a result, I will have a more rigorous test of the sorting hypothesis.

In this chapter, I look at the NES panels from 1972-1974-1976, 1992-1994-1996, and 2000-2002-2004. These are three particularly interesting times to examine sorting. The 1970s mark a period of change in the party system: the South begins to realign in the aftermath of the civil rights movement, and Congress begins to polarize as the elite-level parties become more unified. In the 1990s, we have the continued polarization of Congress, the Republican takeover of Congress in 1994, and President Clinton's return to the center in 1996. Finally, in the 2000s, we have the contested election of 2000 (giving us the famous red-state/blue-state maps) and the September 11th attacks on America, both of which shape the contours of American political life in important ways. In summary, each panel study covers an interesting and politically relevant period in time. By examining a variety of different points in time, I can construct a richer picture of the determinants of sorting.

Testing the Competing Hypotheses

I outlined a variety of testable hypotheses about the determinants of sorting earlier in this chapter. In the panel data analysis, I use the same operationalization of the variables I used in the cross-sectional analysis discussed above, with one exception. For the hypothesis about general political information, I use slightly different measures to take advantage of additional variables that are included in the panel data but are not available in every year of the cross-sectional studies.

To test the hypothesis about the effects of general political information, I use an index of factual knowledge items. This index has two components: civics class items (what is the length of the term of a U.S. senator?) and current political knowledge (which party currently controls the House of Representatives?). While many measures of political knowledge also use the respondent's ability to place the parties on a variety of the NES issue scales (Luskin and Bullock 2006), here I avoid the use of these measures. The reason for this exclusion is that such relative placements are too closely related both conceptually and operationally to another hypothesis discussed in this chapter: the respondent's knowledge of elite polarization.[4] To add relative placements to this index would simply make it nearly impossible to distinguish between these two hypotheses.

Before moving on to discuss the specific model results, I need to say one final word about the data. Here, I want to study the direction of the relationship between recognition of elite party differences and sorting to aid in ultimately determining which variable is the cause and which is the effect. This requires special attention to the timing of respondent changes. Suppose I observe a respondent who is both sorted and recognizes elite polarization at the same point in time. Although I might be able to conclude that there is a relationship between these two variables, determining the direction of that relationship is more vexing: it could be the case that recognition of elite party differences leads to sorting, but the converse (that sorting leads to recognition of elite party differences) is also possible. This is the situation I encountered earlier in the cross-sectional analysis.

The panel data offer me a solution to this problem, however. Suppose I observe a respondent who, at time 1, understands that elites are polarized but who is unsorted. Further suppose that at time 2 said respondent is sorted. Because of the temporal aspect of the panel data, I can more confidently conclude that it is in fact his understanding of elite polarization that leads that respondent to sort, rather than the reverse. Therefore, in the models I estimate using the panel data, I use a one-period lag of each of the independent variables. That is, how does recognition of elite party differences in 1992 affect the probability of being sorted in 1994? Using this strategy, I can more confidently draw inferences about how the various covariates affect a respondent's probability of becoming or remaining sorted.

With those matters out of the way, I can move on to a discussion of the model results. Table 4.1 presents the results from the model estimated from the 1992-1994-1996 panel data. Note that respondents who were previously sorted are much more likely to be sorted in the current period, reflecting the temporal dependence in the data.[5] Beyond the lagged dependent variable, what explains sorting? The model reveals strong sup-

TABLE 4.1 **Panel data model of sorting**

Variable	Estimate
Intercept	**−1.84**
	(0.28)
Sorted in previous period	**2.06**
	(0.13)
Recognize elite party differences	**0.88**
	(0.15)
General political information	**0.36**
	(0.08)
Democrat	0.06
	(0.15)
Male	−0.16
	(0.13)
Pre−New Deal cohort	−0.32
	(0.33)
New Deal cohort	**−0.51**
	(0.21)
Post−New Deal cohort	−0.29
	(0.19)
Baby boomer cohort	−0.22
	(0.16)
Caucasian	**0.44**
	(0.19)
South	0.20
	(0.18)
Lowest third, income	**−0.40**
	(0.16)
Highest third, income	0.11
	(0.15)
Democrat*South	−0.33
	(0.26)
N	1808
ROC	0.85
ROC (null model)	0.78

Note: Logistic regression results predicting whether or not respondents are sorted using the 1992-1994-1996 panel data. The independent variables used are lagged one period: the independent variables are measured in 1992 (1994), and the dependent variable is measured in 1994 (1996). Cell entries are logistic regression coefficients with associated standard errors below in parentheses. Results that can be distinguished from zero at conventional levels of statistical significance (a < 0.10, two-tailed) are given in **bold.**

port for three hypotheses: recognition of elite party differences, general political information, and cohort effects. Recognizing elite polarization has a positive and statistically significant effect on sorting, as predicted. Note that the temporal ordering is more certain here: seeing elite polarization in 1992 generates sorting in 1994, so I can be more confident that I have correctly identified the direction of the relationship. Those who understand in 1992 (1994) that the Democratic Party is more liberal than the Republican Party are more likely to be sorted in 1994 (1996). Taking an otherwise-average respondent (i.e., holding all variables at their mean/median values) and moving him from not seeing party differences to seeing them increases the probability of sorting by almost 16 percent, a large substantive difference.[6] The ideological location of elites provides respondents with valuable information about how to organize their political beliefs.[7]

Additionally, beyond even these regression results, there is support for the sorting hypothesis in the raw data. Contrast two groups of respondents, both of which were unsorted in 1992 and 1994 but were sorted in 1996. In the first group, the respondents could not correctly place the parties in 1992 but could do so in 1994. In the second group, the respondents could not place the parties correctly in either 1992 or 1994. I expect there to be more sorting in the first group: this group had the necessary contextual knowledge in 1994, which should help them sort in 1996. Using this stringent test reveals strong support for my hypothesis: in the first group 25 percent are sorted but only 14 percent are sorted in the second group (the probability that the first group contains more sorted respondents is 0.95; this result comes from using a simulation-based test described in Sekhon 2005). The caveat here is that these are both very small groups of respondents. But that concern aside, this analysis confirms the results from the regression model above: when respondents can correctly place the parties on the liberal-conservative scale, they have the necessary contextual information to align their party and ideology.

Additionally, general political information has a positive and significant effect (a finding that survives even when controlling for the respondent's formal level of education). The more a respondent generally knows about politics, the more likely he is to mimic the elite partisan-ideological alignment and become sorted. This follows fairly directly from the extant literature on the effects of political information, which repeatedly demonstrates that those with high levels of general political information behave the most like elites. Here again, taking an average respondent and increasing his level of general political information from the mean level of information to one standard deviation above the mean increases his probability of being sorting by approximately 9 percent. Although both general political information and recognition of elite polarization have a statistically significant effect on becoming sorted, the effect is larger for recognition of elite polarization. More specifically, the effect of recognition of elite polarization is approximately twice as large as the effect of general political information, so a unit change in recognition in elite polarization has approximately the same effect on the logit scale as a two-unit change in political information. Given the scale of these variables, taking someone from not recognizing elite polarization to recognizing elite polarization is equivalent to increasing the respondent's political information about two standard deviations (here, one unit is equal to one standard deviation on the political information scale; see the appendix for more details). Given the range of political information, this is equivalent to taking someone from approximately the mean level of political information and making him one of the most well informed respondents in the sample. While both recognition of elite party differences and general political information have an effect on becoming sorted, the substantive impact of recognition of elite party differences is much larger than the effect of general political information.

The data also verify that cohort effects are a significant factor driving sorting. In particular, table 4.1 reveals that those in the New Deal cohort (born 1915–1930) are less likely to be sorted (and those in the post–New Deal cohort [born 1931–1955] are marginally less likely to be sorted, $p = 0.11$). Here, these are offsets relative to the baseline cohort, which in this case comprises those under thirty years of age in 1992 (born after 1962). So older voters (born 1915–1931) are less likely to be sorted. This stems from the differences in the elite environment when the two groups came of age politically. The younger voters came of age during the 1980s and 1990s, when the political elites were already becoming more sharply polarized. By contrast, the older voters came of age during the 1940s and 1950s, when elites were more heterogeneous. As a result of these different elite environments, these older voters are less likely to be sorted (Stoker and Jennings 2008).[8]

Interestingly, there is no support for the southern Democrat hypothesis. There is no difference between Democrats and Republicans or between northern and southern Democrats. By the 1990s, then, southern Democrats looked like their northern counterparts, at least in their propensity to be sorted. In supplemental analyses (available in the online appendix), I demonstrate that southern Democrats were less likely to sorted than their northern counterparts in earlier eras (like the 1970s). These differences, however, vanished by the 1990s, suggesting that conditional on other factors, sorting did not differ by region at the end of the twentieth century. So when elites were more heterogeneous, with a distinctive southern Democratic Party, southern Democratic voters were likewise distinctive. But as these elite differences vanished, so did the mass ones.

The control variables have only a modest effect on sorting. Two controls are statistically significant: race and low income. As in the over-time analysis, Caucasian respondents are more likely to be sorted. Low-income voters are also less likely to be sorted. I leave explaining these patterns for future work, simply noting here that, taken as a whole, the demographic factors are somewhat less important determinants of sorting than the attitudinal variables.

Overall, however, this panel analysis yields clear evidence of the determinants of sorting. Given the strength of the prior findings on recognition of elite party differences, it is no surprise that they were handsomely confirmed. However, the results here also suggest that other factors—particularly cohort effects and general political information—matter as well.

What do the results from other panels look like? Do the same sorts of general explanations work there as well? Despite variation in the political environment over time, the basic patterns of results replicate across panels. That is, in the 1972-1974-1976 panel and the 2000-2002-2004 panel, there is strong support for the hypothesis that recognition of elite polarization is a key factor driving sorting. This seems to suggest that the primary substantive effect generalizes beyond just the 1990s (see the online appendix). It appears that elite polarization is more generally related to sorting.

Conclusions

This chapter provides support for one of my key claims: that even controlling for other potential explanations, elite polarization is a major factor behind mass sorting. I have demonstrated this finding both over time with NES cross-sectional data and with NES panel data. The results in both cases are clear and support my theoretical claims. What they cannot support, however, is a *causal* claim: they merely support a claim that elite polarization is *related* to sorting. I turn to the vital task of establishing causality in the next chapter.

CHAPTER FIVE

Untangling the Causes of Sorting

In the previous two chapters I used a variety of observational data to demonstrate that sorting has taken place over the past thirty years and that this change is related to changing levels of elite polarization. This gives me strong real-world support for my primary argument.

These data do not, however, allow me to make any causal claims about the relationship between elite polarization and mass sorting. The data I have used (all observational data) can support only associational claims (e.g., as elite polarization increases, so does mass sorting), not causal ones (e.g., the increase in elite polarization, by clarifying where the parties stand on the issues of the day, causes mass sorting). This is the classic "correlation does not equal causation" issue. As a result, I cannot really be certain that I have correctly identified the causal mechanism behind sorting. The evidence in chapters 3 and 4 is suggestive, but it is not definitive.

This same argument applies equally well to all of the existing work on sorting. All of these studies use over-time (observational) data, which cannot support causal claims, meaning that no prior work can actually speak to the causal (rather than merely correlation) linkage between elite polarization and mass sorting. To correct this shortcoming, I generated experimental data to actually directly test the causal mechanism in question.

The Rise of Stem Cell Research

I begin my study of cause-and-effect relationships by examining the rise of stem cell research. The issue of embryonic stem cell research[1] first emerged on the scene in 1998, with the report from University of Wisconsin researcher Dr. James A. Thomson that he had successfully isolated embryonic stem cells.[2] The original stem cell discovery was ineligible for federal funding under rules banning government support for research involving human embryos. But Thomson's discovery prompted the National Institutes of Health (NIH) to ask the Department of Health and Human Services for a review of the guidelines to see if it would be possible to conduct embryonic stem cell research with federal funds. The Clinton administration issued new regulations in 2000, allowing federal funding of stem cell research (American Association for the Advancement of Science 2004).[3]

In 2001, with George W. Bush in the White House, opponents of the Clinton-era rules pushed to restrict this research. Such a change seemed quite likely given Bush's 2000 campaign pledge to not fund research that involved the destruction of human embryos (Lacayo 2001). In August 2001, President Bush announced new rules for stem cell research, allowing only research on those stem cell lines already in existence (American Association for the Advancement of Science 2004). At the time, the decision was framed primarily as an ethical, rather than a political, issue (Wilgoren and Keller 2004). The president's 2001 address announcing his policy spoke of the "vast ethical mine fields" presented by this type of research and the need to balance a respect for life with the potential for scientific progress (Bush 2001). Indeed, commenting on the president's decision-making process for this policy, Senator Sam Brownback noted that "he [President Bush] was searching more for moral authority than political counsel" (Lacayo 2001).

As a result, response to the president's policy did not fall neatly along partisan lines. Bush's policy attracted strong condemnation from many moderate Republicans, and even some high-profile conservatives—most notably Senators Hatch and Thurmond—spoke out against Bush's policy (Connolly 2001). Divisions within the elite Republican Party, combined with the president's ethical framing of the issue, made it difficult to understand how the stem cell issue mapped onto the partisan divide.

The same cannot be said of the debate during the 2004 presidential campaign, when the issue became defined along more explicitly partisan lines. The Democratic nominee (Senator Kerry) attempted to capitalize on the issue, arguing that President Bush had "turned his back on science" by refusing to fund the research, and promised to reverse this policy once in office. Kerry's pollster, Mark Mellman, argued that Bush's policy was the result of "ideological blinders" and suggested that Bush had caved in to the Religious Right (Milbank and Kurtz 2004). The Democratic convention featured a prime-time speech by former president Reagan's son in an effort to persuade wavering Republicans on the issue (Hillygus and Shields 2008). In response to Senator Kerry's attacks, the president and other key Republican leaders stood by his decision to limit stem cell research and refused to ease restrictions on their use. This sharp differentiation between the parties should have made it much simpler for ordinary Democrats and Republicans to adopt their party's position.

This shift in elite discourse allows me to assess how elite behavior impacts mass attitudes about stem cell research. Prior to the 2004 presidential campaign, the issue was not framed in partisan terms but rather in ethical ones. As a result, variables like religious belief and other demographic factors should largely predict attitudes on stem cell research. In particular, party should bear little relation to these attitudes, because the cues coming from elites were not particularly partisan. After the 2004 election—when the issue became politicized—we should see a much sharper differentiation by party. Given that presidential candidates are among the most visible and important spokespersons for their parties (see the discussion in chapter 2), their positions are the primary partisan and elite cues that ordinary citizens will receive on the issue. In light of the sharp split between the two candidates, we should see partisan affiliation playing a strong role in structuring partisan attitudes post-2004—that is, there should be evidence of partisan sorting on the stem cell issue between 2001 and 2004. This implies a testable hypothesis. Prior to and immediately after Bush's 2001 policy decision, party should be only weakly related to stem cell attitudes, net of other factors. But after the 2004 election, stem cell attitudes should be much more tightly connected to partisanship.

There is one limitation to this design, however. In order to draw any firm inferences about the effects of elite behavior on stem cell attitudes, I need to know that elite opinion leads mass opinion, and not the reverse: it must not be the case that the mass public's attitudes changed, and then elites shifted their positions as a result. There is no evidence that would establish this beyond all reasonable doubt, but there is some evidence suggesting that the direction of causality runs from elites to masses rather than the reverse. During this period, aggregate public opinion remained relatively constant, with approximately 68 percent of the public supporting stem cell research (see below for the data). Further, 2004 campaign coverage suggests that the Kerry campaign realized that President Bush's policy was unattractive to many voters, and if they clarified where the parties stood on the issue, voters would realize they supported the Democrats on this issue (see, e.g., Milbank and Kurtz 2004). The existing data are therefore consistent with the claim that the elites clarified where they stood on the issue and only then did the opinions of the mass public change. Since I cannot definitively establish this point, however, the evidence in this section may not be enough by itself to establish causality. Nevertheless, combined with other types of evidence presented later in the chapter, it does offer me a compelling test of my theory.

To test my sorting hypothesis, I need data on respondents' positions on stem cell research before and after the 2004 election. This information comes from the polling data gathered by the *Washington Post* and ABC News. These groups regularly conduct polls of Americans on a variety of different topics, and they asked about stem cell research at two different points in time: in late July 2001 (prior to the president's announcement of the policy limiting stem cell research) and in early June 2005 (after the partisan divide on the issue in 2004).[4] Luckily, these two studies used the same item to measure support for stem cell research, so I can explore how changes in elite positions affect mass attitudes. Table 5.1 shows the results predicting support for stem cell research at both points in time.[5]

In 2001, party identification had little bearing on whether or not one supported stem cell research. In fact, aside from liberal-conservative self-identification (which strongly predicts attitudes toward stem cell research, with conservatives being more opposed), it is the demographic variables that seem to structure attitudes toward stem cell research. The strong opposition among Catholics and evangelicals should come as no surprise: given that this research involves destroying embryos (which these faiths teach are living human beings) to harvest the stem cells, this research runs afoul of basic moral tenets of these faiths.[6] I do not have a specific theory about why income and education should affect attitudes about stem cell research; perhaps they proxy for familiarity with science and research more generally. But overall, demographics—not partisan affiliation—structured attitudes toward stem cell research in 2001.

TABLE 5.1 **Sorting on stem cell research**

Variable	2001	2005
Intercept	**1.54**	**1.82**
	(0.55)	(0.69)
Party identification	−0.0002	**−0.31**
	(0.04)	(0.06)
Liberal-conservative self-identification	**−0.53**	**−0.51**
	(0.11)	(0.13)
College graduate	**0.47**	0.11
	(0.16)	(0.19)
Age	−0.02	0.27
	(0.22)	(0.29)
Age-squared	0.002	−0.009
	(0.02)	(0.03)
Catholic	**−0.56**	**−0.95**
	(0.17)	(0.21)
Evangelical	**−0.96**	**−1.4**
	(0.16)	(0.19)
Income	**0.26**	**0.27**
	(0.08)	(0.09)
N	1110	835
ROC	0.71	0.79

Note: Logistic regression results predicting support for stem cell research in 2001 and 2005 samples. Coefficients that are statistically different from zero at conventional levels are indicated in **bold**. Note that here age is divided by 10 to give more easily interpretable coefficient estimates. The results in this table and the text are based on unweighted data. Exact question wordings and response options are given in the appendix.

Although demographics, particularly religion, matter in 2005, party is now a major explanatory factor underlying support for stem cell research. The null hypothesis that the effect of party is equal across the two years can be rejected at the $p = 0.01$ (two-tailed) level. In 2005, moving from leaning Democrat to leaning Republican lowers the probability of support by 8 percent, all else equal, and the parallel move from Democrat to Republican decreases the probability of support by 15 percent. Indeed, just looking at the raw data, the difference in support between Democrats and Republicans for stem cell research was 8 percent in 2001 but grew to 26 percent in 2005 as the two sides sorted themselves out. For example, Democrats became 9 percent more supportive of stem cell research while Republicans became 9 percent more opposed. These results suggest strong support for my sorting hypothesis: when partisan elites take clear and distinct positions on the issues, mass partisans will sort.[7]

The variation in elite polarization on stem cell research induced by the 2004 campaign allows me to put my findings on a firmer footing. As elites pulled apart ideologically on this issue, ordinary voters took their cues from their elites and aligned their own party and views on stem cell research. This helps to support my claim of a causal link between elite polarization and mass sorting.

Establishing Causality through Experimentation

While the case of stem cell research is suggestive, the lack of a definitive exogenous shift may limit my ability to draw causal inferences from that analysis. To overcome this limitation, I turn to a randomized experiment.[8] The ideal test of my theory would be to randomly assign some voters to a world with highly polarized elites, and others to an identical world with less polarized elites, and observe the difference in sorting. Obviously, this sort of test is impossible. But I can indirectly simulate it with an experiment.

My experiment is a three-condition between-subjects experiment. Subjects were told that we wanted their opinion on a series of policy issues. Subjects were initially given a background paragraph describing an issue. What they then saw varied by treatment condition (treatment assignment was held constant across issues for all subjects).[9] Subjects assigned to the control condition saw no additional information and were simply asked for their opinion on the issue. Subjects in the two treatment conditions, however, were given information about elite positions before being asked for their opinion. Subjects were provided with the positions of members of Congress on each issue (subjects were told that the information came from a scientific study of members of Congress conducted by an official government agency; see the appendix for more details). The assumption here is that the positions of members of Congress represent the positions of the national parties as a whole, a reasonable assumption frequently used in past research (see, e.g., Carmines and Stimson 1989, McCarty, Poole, and Rosenthal 2006).

The two treatment conditions differed only in their level of polarization. In the polarized elites (high polarization) condition, the parties were ideologically distinct from one another and were relatively internally ideologically homogeneous (e.g., Democrats are liberals, Republicans are conservatives, and there is essentially no overlap between the two). Elites in this polarized elites condition essentially mimicked the elites of the 1990s and 2000s. In the other treatment condition, the moderate elites (low polarization) condition, elites looked more like they did in the 1960s and

1970s. The parties were more heterogeneous (e.g., some Democrats are conservative, and some Republicans are liberal), and the parties' positions were less ideologically distinct from one another (for the specific stimuli viewed by the respondents, see the online appendix). Comparing subjects' behavior in these two conditions allowed me to draw inferences about the effect of elite polarization on citizens' attitudes.

Note that, in keeping with the theoretical discussion in chapter 2, "polarization" consists of two factors in my experiment: the ideological homogeneity of the parties and the ideological distance between the parties. In an ideal experiment, I would have manipulated each dimension of polarization (homogeneity and distance) separately; sample size constraints prevented me from doing so here. I accept this as a necessary limitation of the current design and leave parsing out the distinct effects of each factor for future work. I simply note in passing that there are no specific hypotheses in the extant literature about the independent effects of homogeneity versus ideological distance, so this is a case where both additional theorizing and additional analysis are needed. For now, I am content to simply comment on the effect of "polarization" (the combination of both homogeneity and ideological distance) on voter attitudes (for more discussion of this point, see Levendusky 2008).

For my experiment to be successful, I needed to manipulate respondents' perceptions of elite polarization (and then examine whether these different perceptions of polarization affected sorting). I included a manipulation check in my survey instrument to assess whether or not my experimental manipulation changed respondents' beliefs about elite polarization. After the experimental stimulus described above, I asked respondents to rate the degree of similarity or difference in the positions taken by Democrats and Republicans. If my experimental manipulation functioned as intended, then subjects assigned to the polarized elites condition should perceive greater differences between the parties' positions than subjects in the other two conditions. A one-way ANOVA confirms this intuition ($F(2, 8599) = 9.7, p < 0.01$). While only 24 percent of subjects assigned to the moderate elites condition thought the parties' positions were "very different," 49 percent of subjects in the polarized elites condition felt this way (as did 22 percent of subjects in the control condition). Simply put, voters perceive greater differences between the parties when they are depicted as more polarized. So the manipulation functioned as intended: subjects assigned to the different experimental conditions perceived different levels of elite polarization. My experiment therefore put me in a strong position to test the key substantive hypothesis of interest: when subjects perceive higher levels of elite polarization, do they exhibit higher levels of sorting?

My claim is not, however, that voters in the real world receive the sorts of cues given in this experiment; my stimuli are necessarily artificial. The key point is that they simulate the empirical phenomenon of interest: when elites are more polarized, voters perceive greater differences between the parties. In the real world, the ways in which voters learn about the parties' positions are obviously more complex than these simple cues (see chapter 2). But the fact remains that voters *do* learn about the degree of elite polarization, and as elites' positions become more polarized, voters perceive elites to offer more distinctive policy alternatives (see chapter 3). My stimuli therefore simulate the actual process of interest in the real world: when voters perceive greater elite polarization (for whatever reason or by whatever means), are they then more likely to sort?[10]

To give the most compelling test possible of my theory, the items used here were selected according to three primary criteria. First, I chose items about which I expected subjects to have only weak prior beliefs. This ensures that my experimental manipulation—and not the respondent's preexisting opinion—is the key source of information about the issue. This ruled out, for example, high-profile issues like the war in Iraq, abortion, same-sex marriage, and so forth. Second, I also excluded issues that were so obscure that respondents would have no real basis for opinion formation. To that end, I selected my issues from the lists of "key votes" generated by research organizations (e.g., Project Vote Smart, *Congressional Quarterly, National Journal*) and interest groups (e.g., the AFL-CIO, Sierra Club, Chamber of Commerce), thereby ensuring that the issues in the survey were not irrelevant to the larger political debate. Finally, I also eliminated issues that were extremely popular (or unpopular) to avoid any floor or ceiling effects, which ruled out issues like prescription drug importation or outsourcing.

Specifically, I selected five issues for this experiment: (1) whether the Army Corps of Engineers should add more external review of the environmental impact of a project prior to construction, (2) whether air traffic controllers should remain federal government employees or instead be employed by private firms, (3) whether the government should permit deregulation of the electricity market, (4) whether the government should maintain the ban on coastal drilling for oil and natural gas, and (5) whether the federal or state governments should maintain primary control over job-training programs (see the appendix for specific item wordings). These issues are obscure enough that subjects were likely to have weak opinions about them but still tap into broader political debates about government intervention into the economy, the trade-off between economic growth and environmental protection, and federalism.

One might be tempted to argue that opinion formation on these sorts of less salient issues is inherently uninteresting, but this view is short-sighted. If I had selected more salient issues (e.g., Iraq, same-sex marriage), then I would have been unable to manipulate respondents' beliefs about the parties' positions, and hence would have been unable to test the causal mechanism in my theory. Low-salience issues, in contrast, allow a much more straightforward test of my theory.

These less salient issues are also important in their own right. They simulate opinion formation on a new issue as it rises to prominence on the political agenda, when ordinary voters do not yet know where they—or even elites—stand on the issue. My experimental results clarify how attitudes become sorted on emerging issues.[11] For more crystallized and familiar issues, I would not expect to find these patterns of elite effects, at least not on an ongoing basis. But this brings up an important design point: if I want to estimate the effect of elites on mass opinion, much of that effect is concentrated in the early stages of issue emergence. So to understand how elites shape voter sorting, I need to study novel issues; studying more salient issues misses the majority of the elite effects. The logic of this design directly parallels Bartels's (1993) arguments about media effects: in order to understand what happens on more salient issues, we need to study more obscure ones.

These experiments were embedded in a nationally representative survey conducted with Knowledge Networks in November 2007. Knowledge Networks is a leading Internet survey firm with a unique twist. Most Internet samples suffer from a serious design flaw: because the respondents consist of volunteer panelists and not a random sample of households, the conclusions from a particular sample do not necessarily generalize to the larger U.S. population. Knowledge Networks, however, recruits panelists via random-digit-dialing (RDD) telephone methods and then administers the surveys online through a webTV unit given to panelists. The Knowledge Networks data are therefore a random sample of American households, and my conclusions will generalize to the general U.S. population. The quality of data from Knowledge Networks samples compares favorably to that of standard RDD telephone samples (Krosnick and Chang 2001), and data from Knowledge Networks have been widely used throughout political science (see, among many others, Huber and Lapinski 2006; Jackman and Hillygus 2003; Clinton 2006).

While the Knowledge Networks sample is generalizable to the entire population, there is one limitation with my sample. I deliberately excluded pure independents (those who do not lean toward one party or the other) from my sample.[12] I did so on theoretical grounds: my hypotheses are about how partisans will respond to party cues, and as a result, I lack any clear expectation about how independents will respond to these party cues. My results are therefore generalizable only to the population of partisans; I leave it to future work to consider how independents are affected by these sorts of cues.

Does Elite Polarization Cause Sorting?

If my theory is correct, then I should find that in the high polarization condition more respondents are sorted than in the low polarization or control conditions. But how should I operationalize sorting in this experiment? Throughout the book, I have argued that sorted respondents take the same position on the issue as their party's elites. In these experiments, the key difference in elite positions between the high and low polarization conditions is the location of the modal elite: in the high polarization case, the modal elite strongly agrees/disagrees, whereas in the low polarization case, they only agree/disagree with the policy (see the stimuli in the online appendix). Therefore, I expect to find more respondents selecting the "strongly agree" or "strongly disagree" options in the high polarization condition. As a result, I say a respondent is sorted if he strongly agrees or strongly disagrees with the policy (depending upon his party identification). If my argument is correct, then I expect to find more sorting—that is, more respondents taking the strongly agree/disagree positions—in the high polarization condition. To test this hypothesis, I pooled across issues and ran a logistic regression as a function of treatment assignment, issue-specific fixed effects (to control for difference by issue), and subject-specific random effects (to control for unmodeled differences in subject-specific propensity to be sorted); similar results can be obtained using ANOVA. Table 5.2 gives the results.

Table 5.2 provides strong causal evidence in support of my theory that elite polarization causes sorting. Here, the interest centers on the interpretation of the treatment effect coefficients. The "control condition" and "high polarization condition" coefficients are offsets measuring the differ-

TABLE 5.2 **Experimental evidence for sorting**

Variable	Estimate
Intercept	**0.15**
	(0.01)
Control condition	0.007
	(0.01)
High polarization condition	**0.05**
	(0.01)
Includes Issue Fixed Effects	
Includes Subject Random Effects	
N	8815

Note: Logistic regression predicting sorting as a function of treatment assignment, issue-specific fixed effects, and subject-specific random effects. Coefficients that are statistically distinguishable from zero are given in **bold.**

ence between sorting in that condition relative to the omitted category, the low polarization condition.[13] Table 5.2 reveals that while there is no difference in sorting between the control and the low polarization condition, there is a difference between the low and the high polarization condition. So when elites are more ideologically divided, respondents are more likely to be sorted—here, about 4–5 points on average, a finding that emerges from simply examining the raw data as well. My experiments demonstrate strong support for the causal logic underlying my argument in this book: when elites take more polarized positions, voters notice these changes, and as a result, voters are more likely to adopt their party's position on the issues.

But overall, the results of my experiments strengthen the analysis offered in earlier sections by demonstrating a *causal* linkage between elite polarization and mass sorting. Rather than merely making associational claims, these results allow me to make causal ones: as elites pull apart and clarify where they stand on the issues, ordinary voters will sort. It is clear that, while other factors clearly matter for sorting (see the discussion of the panel data above), these results demonstrate that elite polarization has a direct causal effect on mass sorting.

Conclusions

This chapter puts the elite polarization–sorting linkage on much firmer footing than past research has permitted. Using experimental data I demonstrated a causal link between changes in elite polarization and mass sorting. These experiments allow me to go beyond previous research, which can offer only an associational claim about the effects of elites on masses. Possessing this casual evidence becomes particularly important in light of some of the criticisms discussed in chapter 3. For example, some critics of sorting argue that, because sorting varies by issue and many voters remain unsorted despite high levels of elite polarization, changes in citizens' recognition of elite polarization cannot directly cause sorting. But my experimental results show that this belief is incorrect—elite polarization does cause mass sorting. Future work will be needed to refine these estimates and examine how these findings extend to other issues, other variants of treatment, and so on. But these results establish a minimum baseline that a direct relationship exists between elite polarization and mass sorting.

CHAPTER SIX

How Voters Sort

In the preceding chapters, I provided the theoretical and empirical justification for *why* voters sort: as elites pull apart ideologically, they clarify where the parties stand on the issues of the day. Voters then use these clearer party cues to align their own partisan and ideological beliefs. But *how* do voters sort? Imagine that an unsorted voter—say a conservative Democrat—decides to sort. He has two options. He could adjust his ideological beliefs to fit with his partisanship by becoming a liberal Democrat; I term this party-driven sorting. Or he could change his partisanship to fit with his ideological beliefs and become a conservative Republican; I term this ideology-driven sorting. Which of these pathways—party-driven or ideology-driven sorting—is more prominent in the mass electorate? This chapter explores the theoretical and empirical support for each type of sorting.

The Party-Driven Model of Sorting

Suppose respondents sort by moving their ideology into alignment with their party identification (ID).[1] This suggests a model of political behavior in which partisanship is the dominant influence on ordinary citizens' behavior, whereas ideology is somewhat more malleable. Nearly fifty years of scholarship on political behavior builds upon a model of political behavior with a long-term, stable partisanship at its core (Campbell et al. 1980; Miller and Shanks 1996). Indeed, according to this view, party ID is the unmoved mover: the long-term, stable force that shapes "attitudes toward political objects" (Campbell et al. 1980, 135). Partisan ID is at the core of citizens' political identities and fundamentally influences how they see the political world. It develops fairly early in life, is stable over time, and is relatively resistant to change from outside forces such as issue positions. Consistent with this view, once measurement error is removed, partisanship is remarkably stable over time (Green, Palmquist, and Schickler 2002).

According to this point of view, party ID raises a "perceptual screen" that biases individuals' view of the world and how they assimilate new information. Recent work on partisan bias suggests that party ID powerfully affects any number of aspects of citizens' political behavior and attitudes (Achen and Bartels 2006; Bartels 2000, 2002; Goren 2005; however, for an alternative, dissenting view, see Gerber and Green 1998, 1999). Even seemingly neutral factual items (e.g., whether or not the budget deficit increased or decreased during President Reagan's tenure in office) are subject to strong partisan biases (Bartels 2002). Partisanship's ability to influence how citizens see the political world is both substantial and ubiquitous.

In contrast to the stability of partisanship, ideology is more malleable— much of the time, coherent ideological reasoning is beyond the capability of most voters, even on long-standing, salient issues of public policy (Converse 1964). Most voters simply do not think about politics and political issues enough to possess the well-developed abstract belief systems characteristic of elites (however, for an alternative view, see Ansolabehere, Rodden, and Snyder 2008).

If this is the case, how can citizens ever hope to hold a coherent set of positions on the issues? The usual answer is that they need outside help. The most obvious place for citizens to look is to political elites, who help voters make sense of the political world and the issues of the day (Brody 1991; Zaller 1992; Jacoby 1988). Ordinary voters cannot form coherent views on a long list of issues, but they can look to elites for guidance on what positions they should take. Elites allow ordinary voters to have at least a general sense of where they should stand on contemporary issues.

According to this theory, sorting occurs because ordinary citizens think: "I'm a Democrat. What do Democrats think about issue X?" They then look at where elite Democrats stand on issue X and adopt that position as their own. This mode of thinking is similar to the processing described in the party cues literature. There, the typical finding is that when presented with a party cue ("The Democratic Party supports position X on issue Y") citizens will be much more likely to bring their own thinking into alignment with their party's position (see, e.g., Rahn 1993; Bullock 2006; Cohen 2003). The process here is the same: to sort, voters adopt their party's position on the issues. Party ID provides citizens with a powerful heuristic to use to understand the political world and the issues of the day.

The Ideology-Driven Model of Sorting

On the other hand, suppose voters sort by keeping their ideology constant and adjusting their party ID to fit with their ideology. This suggests a model in which party ID is not an unmoved mover but rather responds to an individual's issue positions and to changes in the political world (Fiorina 1981). Here party ID is seen as a "running tally" of an individual's experiences with the parties; as people's experiences with the parties change, so does their party ID (Franklin and Jackson 1983; Brody and Rothenberg 1988; Franklin 1984). Although party ID is generally stable, it responds to the ebb and flow of the political world.

Given a substantial shift in the political environment, issue positions may even lead individuals to switch parties. For example, this is the classic explanation for the twentieth-century southern realignment: conservative Democrats became conservative Republicans as the Democratic Party pulled to the left on a host of issues (Gerber and Jackson 1993; Carmines and Stimson 1989). Some even argue that these issue-driven shifts provide the basis of mass realignments of the party system (Schattschneider 1960; Sundquist 1983; Key 1955; Riker 1986). In contrast to the party-driven model of sorting, it is ideology and related issue positions, not partisanship, that are the dominant causal factor (Page and Jones 1979; Markus and Converse 1979).[2]

How does this ideology-driven sorting work? A voter has opinions about the issues of the day and then asks: "I think X about issue Y. Which party's position is closest to X?" The voter examines the parties' positions and identifies with the party whose position most clearly matches his own. Party ID therefore becomes a summary of a voter's various issue positions (Downs 1957).

One potential problem with this model of sorting, however, is that it rests upon citizens' having stable and well-articulated ideologies, strong enough to change a long-term, stable partisan identification. Yet we also know that most citizens routinely fall short of this standard (Converse 1964; Bartels 2003). Some citizens, however, *do* have the stable and well-thought-out beliefs necessary to alter a partisan identification: issue publics, groups of citizens who are well informed and care deeply about a particular issue (Converse 1964; Krosnick 1990). For these individuals, exiting a party due to their issue positions is quite plausible. For example, many conservative Democratic activists became Republicans once the national Democratic Party pulled to the left in the 1970s and 1980s (Stone, Rapoport, and Abramowitz 1994; Clark et al. 1991). In such cases, partisanship bends to issue beliefs.

Observable Implications of the Two Paths

Voters can sort either by adjusting their ideological beliefs to fit with their partisanship or by adjusting their partisanship to fit with their ideological beliefs. If the party-driven model is correct, when I examine respondents who move from not sorted to sorted, I should observe them changing their ideology rather than their party ID. If the ideology-driven model is correct, I should observe the opposite path: respondents changing their party ID to fit with their ideological beliefs.

But which path do I expect to be more common in the mass electorate? Scholars typically agree that partisanship sits at the center of a voter's worldview and is both influential and highly stable. In order to shift this stable partisanship, voters will need a well-developed, crystallized ideological orientation. Yet acquiring such an orientation is beyond the capabilities of ordinary voters (Converse 1964; Bartels 2003; Jacoby 1995), which casts doubt on self-identification as a driving force for sorting. Additionally, after correcting for measurement error, partisanship is remarkably stable over time (Green, Palmquist, and Schickler 2002). Given this, it seems more likely that a relatively constant factor like party ID drives change in the more flexible ideological identification (Miller 2000). Indeed, looking at opinion change more generally, Carsey and Layman (2006) find that, most typically, ideology bends to accommodate partisanship. So in the specific case of sorting, I expect ideological self-identification to be adjusted to fit with partisanship.

Although I expect most sorting to be party driven, this may not be the case for the most politically informed respondents. These respondents are the most likely to have coherent, stable belief systems structured along ideological lines (Converse 1964). Given the power and stability of party ID, only a coherent and well-developed belief system should lead to ideology-driven partisan change. I therefore expect ideology-driven sorting to be limited to highly politically sophisticated respondents.

Testing These Models of Sorting

To test whether party or ideology is the dominant factor driving sorting, I examine how respondents move from unsorted to sorted using the NES panel data introduced in earlier chapters. I expect to find that most sorting is party driven—that most respondents who sort do so by changing their ideological beliefs to fit with their partisanship. Table 6.1 test this hypothesis using data from the 1992-1994-1996 NES panel data.[3]

The data strongly support this hypothesis. Take, for example, sorting on the liberal-conservative scale. Almost twice as many voters follow the party-driven route as follow the ideology-driven one: 53 percent sort by changing their liberal-conservative self-identification (e.g., go from a conservative Democrat to a liberal Democrat), but only 28 percent sort by changing their partisanship (e.g., change from a liberal Republican to a liberal Democrat); the remaining 19 percent change both factors at the same time (e.g., go from a moderate independent to a conservative Republican). Looking across issues, there is typically considerably more party-driven sorting than ideology-driven sorting; the same pattern extends to the 1994-1996 wave of the data (omitted from table 6.1 in the interest of space). Sorting is primarily party driven.

TABLE 6.1 **Party-driven versus ideology-driven sorting**

Issue	Change Issue Position (%)	Change Party (%)	Change Both (%)
Liberal-conservative self-identification	53	28	19
Guaranteed jobs	61	29	11
Abortion	44	49	6
Government services and spending	71	16	13
Defense spending	71	15	14
Aid to minorities	65	26	9
Government vs. private health insurance	63	26	12

Note: Respondents sort by changing their position on the issue, their partisanship, or both factors. The data come from the 1992–1994 waves of the 1992-1994-1996 panel data.

The only exception to this pattern is for legalized abortion, where there is slightly more ideology-driven change than party-driven change. If there is one issue where I would expect more ideology-driven change, it would be abortion: it is an "easy" issue (Carmines and Stimson 1980), is extremely salient, and is discussed frequently by both politicians and the media. So this is the type of issue where even marginally informed voters should be able to form the type of stable, coherent attitudes needed to change partisanship. With only one issue, this reasoning is necessarily speculative, but it does suggest that the type of issue may influence whether partisanship or issue position is the more malleable factor; I leave exploring this hypothesis for future work.

The Effects of Education

The theoretical discussion above made it clear that this general pattern may not hold for all respondents. In particular, I expect that more politically sophisticated respondents—who have the capacity to understand politics in ideological terms—will display higher levels of ideology-driven sorting. Table 6.2 compares party-driven and ideology-driven sorting on the liberal-conservative scale. It does so for both high- and low-education respondents, on the expectation that better-educated respondents will be more likely to understand politics in ideological terms and hence sort by changing their party. Here, education functions as a proxy for political sophistication; using a direct sophistication measure yields similar results.

The evidence here reinforces the conclusion from table 6.1—overall, sorting is party driven. Surprisingly, education—or any other measure of political sophistication—plays no conditioning role. I expected that high-education respondents (here, those who have completed at least some college) would be more likely to sort by changing their partisanship—these are the respondents who are most likely to possess the stable and coherent ideological beliefs needed to drive a change in partisanship. But regardless of a voter's level of education, he is more likely to sort via the party-driven route than the ideology-driven one.

Looking at the other panel datasets, we see the same pattern of results: sorting is primarily driven by changes in ideology. While the pattern may be stronger/weaker for different levels of political sophistication, the basic pattern is the same. I find similar results for items other than the liberal-conservative self-identification scale, suggesting that the results are not simply an artifact of using that particular item. This seems to suggest that the mechanism underlying sorting is only weakly conditional on the

TABLE 6.2 **Effects of education on sorting**

High Education (1992–1994)		
Ideology Driven	No	Yes
Party Driven		
No	—	49
Yes	31	20

Low Education (1992–1994)		
Ideology Driven	No	Yes
Party Driven		
No	—	58
Yes	27	15

High Education (1994–1996)		
Ideology Driven	No	Yes
Party Driven		
No	—	69
Yes	11	19

Low Education (1994–1996)		
Ideology Driven	No	Yes
Party Driven		
No	—	67
Yes	20	13

Note: Cell entries are percentages. For party-driven sorting (ideology-driven sorting), the "No" entries represent cases where party (ideology) was not responsible for the sorting. The "Yes" entries indicate that change in partisanship (ideology) was responsible for the sorting. Note that, in all cases, no one is in a "No/No" cell, because one cannot move from not sorted to sorted without changing either one's partisanship or one's ideology. The cutoff for the high-education group is those who have at least some college education. Changing the cutoff to those who hold at least a bachelor's degree does not substantively alter the results.

political environment and the respondent's level of political information. When individuals bring their party ID and ideology into alignment with each other, they seem to move their ideology, regardless of the political environment or level of elite polarization. Even as the political environment changes, the process of voter change stays the same.[4]

Sorting in the White South

This discussion appears to contradict the explanation of the most famous example of sorting in American history: the transformation of the South over the second half of the twentieth century (Black and Black 2002). While tables 6.1 and 6.2 argue that sorting is party driven, the southern realignment was ideologically driven: conservative southern Democrats abandoned the Democratic Party beginning in the 1960s as the Democratic

TABLE 6.3 **Effects of region on sorting**

White South (1972–1974)			
Ideology Driven		No	Yes
Party Driven	No	—	52
	Yes	44	4

Other Voters (1972–1974)			
Ideology Driven		No	Yes
Party Driven	No	—	73
	Yes	17	11

White South (1974–1976)			
Ideology Driven		No	Yes
Party Driven	No	—	41
	Yes	32	27

Other Voters (1974–1976)			
Ideology Driven		No	Yes
Party Driven	No	—	72
	Yes	18	11

Note: This table replicates table 6.2 for the 1972-1974-1976 panel data, breaking down the data by whether or not the respondent is a white Southerner.

Party moved to the left on racial, defense, and social-welfare policy (Carmines and Stimson 1989; Abramowitz 1994). Can I account for these existing patterns of results within the confines of my study?

If the previous literature is correct, then ideology-driven party exit should be more common among white southerners (those from the states of the former Confederacy) than in the rest of the nation during the 1960s, 1970s, and 1980s. The 1972-1974-1976 panel data allow me to test this hypothesis; table 6.3 gives the results. Although the data reveal that changing liberal-conservative self-identification is always the most common route to sorting regardless of region, ideology-driven change is more common in the white South. Looking at cases where we can attribute sorting to either partisan or ideological change, there is significantly more sorting due to party exit in the white South than in the remainder of the nation ($\alpha < 0.10$, two-tailed). This result, however, does not replicate in later panels (e.g., the 1992-1994-1996 or the 2000-2002 panel). This suggests that, when the South was experiencing a partisan realignment in the 1970s and 1980s, conservative Democrats became conservative Republicans rather than liberal Democrats. But as the white South began to resemble the remainder of the nation in the 1990s (Black and Black 2002), that distinctiveness vanished.

This suggests an important addendum to my earlier conclusions. Under normal circumstances, sorting is party driven, but this pattern does not hold when there are unique elite-level circumstances. So the political context matters, but it matters in a particular way: when elites make it easier to act based on ideology voters will do so. Otherwise, party ID is the dominant factor behind sorting.

More General Patterns

What about the role of partisanship and ideological factors in the more general case of "cross-pressured" partisans? Do we see the same patterns as in the sorting case? I have conducted a series of analyses of cross-pressured partisans—respondents whose issue positions are out of step with their partisan identification (e.g., a pro-life Democrat). Rather than simply examining sorting, I asked whether these respondents reduce the tension between their partisanship and their issue position. So, for example, while a pro-life Democrat may not become a pro-choice Democrat, he might move in that direction (or, alternatively, become more Republican). The findings here replicate my earlier findings: if citizens adjust their beliefs, they do so by changing their issue positions to fit with their partisanship. These findings reinforce earlier results from Carsey and Layman (2006), who find that when voters change their party or ideology, it is almost always their party that is the dominant factor (see also Miller 2000).[5] These findings are available in the online appendix.

A Caveat

While the findings in this chapter provide strong support for the argument that sorting is typically (though not exclusively) party driven, a caveat to these findings is in order. Much of the apparent stability of party ID relative to other political attitudes stems from question format (Krosnick and Berent 1993). The NES asks about respondents' partisanship using a branching format[6] with all response options fully labeled, both of which increase the over-time stability of attitude reports in surveys (Krosnick and Berent 1993). By contrast, ideological self-placement is asked with all response options fully labeled but is not branched. Issue positions are measured without branching and with only the endpoints labeled. I cannot therefore rule out the possibility that with better measures of ideological self-identification and issue positions my results might change. That said, in light of fifty years of political behavior research and the theoretical discussion earlier, I still strongly suspect that party ID is the dominant factor behind sorting. Given available data, however, I cannot definitively prove this, though this deficiency does point to an interesting possibility for future work (namely, running a panel study with all items asked the same way to resolve this measurement quandary). I stress that this problem is not unique to my study—any study using the NES or any other existing over-time data falls prey to the same problem. The entire literature on the stability of party ID should be read with this limitation in mind.

Beyond even this measurement quandary, there is a deeper problem with trying to determine whether party or ideology drives sorting. There is no real way to rigorously test the causal processes underlying these partisan versus ideological change theories. The only data available come from observational studies, so there cannot be any firm claims about causality absent stringent additional assumptions. No natural experiments or survey experiments exist to test these claims, and it is not clear whether such an experiment would even be possible. My results may be consistent with a causal claim, but they cannot definitively prove it.

One approach to try and establish causal claims would be to use a structural equation model estimated with some sort of analysis of covariance software such as LISREL or AMOS. Unfortunately, one cannot establish causality with these types of models without accepting a host of untestable (and, frankly, untenable) assumptions (Freedman 2005; Achen 2000, 2002). Ultimately, I can at best say that my results—along with considerable political science theory and empirical data—are more consistent with a party-dominant model. But I cannot rule out, in light of the caveat mentioned above, that some of this finding is due to the differences in measurement error between party ID and ideology. There is no way to resolve this question through statistical technique; this is an issue that will require new data. Until then, the conclusions above are about all that can be said.

Conclusion

I have presented evidence in this chapter that demonstrates that sorting is party driven: when a respondent moves from unsorted to sorted, he is much more likely to move his ideological beliefs into alignment with his partisanship than the reverse, strongly suggesting that party is the key causal variable. Issue positions or ideology are able to overcome the stability of partisan identification only in special circumstances. In a changing political environment—such as the southern realignment of the mid–twentieth century—sorting is more likely to be driven by party exit rather than ideological change. Beyond that, changing one's partisanship is a fairly limited phenomenon: fairly extraordinary circumstances are needed to overcome the marked stability of partisan identification (Carsey and Layman 2006). Stability in party ID is the norm, squaring with the half century of work consistently finding that party is the dominant impact on citizen behavior.

The marked importance of partisanship highlights two more general conclusions about American politics. First, it highlights the role of parties in structuring American politics. In the United States, elite competition is partisan competition: Democrats and Republicans define the issues of the day and set the terms of the debate. When we see them quoted on TV or in the newspaper, elites are referenced as "Hillary Clinton, Democrat" or "Mike Enzi, Republican." While this may seem trivial, it is not: it underscores that, for ordinary citizens, party is how they understand the political world. Politics in America is organized along partisan lines, and this fact governs how ordinary citizens understand the political world.

Second and as a consequence of the above, party is much more central and concrete for most people. We know that, for most citizens, ideology is an abstract and nebulous concept. The average voter is not interested enough in politics to expend the cognitive resources needed to think in ideological terms. Party, by contrast—in large part because parties structure the terms of the debate in American politics—is much more concrete and real. When people say "I'm a Democrat," people have some idea of what that means. For most people, saying "I'm a conservative" is a much more hazy and abstract conception. Party is more concrete for most respondents, so we should not be surprised that it is at the center of their understanding of the political world. Party elites structure the terms of the debate along partisan lines, and as a result, ordinary citizens respond in partisan terms. Party ID has such a powerful effect because this is the primary method of organizing political competition in American politics (Sniderman and Levendusky 2007).

CHAPTER SEVEN

The Impact of the Sorted

I began this book with a question: why has the mass electorate changed so dramatically over the past forty years? I demonstrated that, as a result of elite polarization, more voters have sorted: that is, voters today are more likely to share the ideological outlook of their national party elites than they were a generation ago. Elite polarization causes sorting by clarifying where the parties stand on the issues of the day. As elites pull apart and take distinct positions on the issues, they send voters clearer signals about the issue positions Democrats and Republicans hold. Voters then use these clearer cues to sort.

This increase in sorting is driven both by existing voters aligning their partisanship and ideology (i.e., a conversion effect) and by younger voters being more likely to enter the electorate already sorted (i.e., a replacement effect). Further, though there has been a large increase in sorting, there has been only a modest increase in polarization. So while the electorate is much better sorted today than it was a generation ago, it is only slightly more polarized, and much of that increased polarization is a direct result of sorting.

In addition to evidence from over-time survey data, I also provide the first experimental evidence linking elite polarization and sorting. Although it is clear using over-time survey data that sorting has increased over the past few decades, prior scholarship could not establish a causal link. My evidence allows me to move beyond association to causation and provides strong support for an elite polarization/mass sorting link.

But what impact does this sorting have on individual voters? When an individual moves from unsorted to sorted, does this change his voting behavior? His evaluation of the parties? His issue positions? Prior scholarship provides very little guidance on these questions. Although a number of scholars have documented some important consequences of sorting, they have tended to focus on topics like realignment theory (Layman and Carsey 2002a; Campbell 2006a). Much less is known about how sorting changes voters themselves. I take up this vital task below.

How Sorting Changes Voters

To begin, consider the effect of sorting on voting behavior. Imagine the complicated choice an unsorted voter faces when he steps into the voting booth—his partisanship and ideological beliefs pull him in opposite directions. These unsorted voters are the classic "cross-pressured" voters, pulled between two competing allegiances (Berelson, Lazarsfeld, and McPhee 1954; Campbell et al. 1980; Miller and Shanks 1996). Take, for example, a conservative Democrat in the 2004 presidential election. His partisanship pulled him toward Senator Kerry, but his ideological beliefs pushed him toward President Bush. His ultimate decision—Kerry or Bush, Democrat or Republican—depended upon the strength of these competing factors. In contrast, had he been sorted, his decision calculus would have been much simpler: partisanship and ideology reinforce one another for sorted voters. Sorting, by reducing a voter's cross-pressures, makes him more likely to support his party at the ballot box (Hillygus and Shields 2008; Carmines and Ensley 2004). This implies two testable hypotheses. First, sorted voters should be more likely to support their same-party presidential nominee. Second, they should also be less likely to split their ticket.

To test these predictions, I turn to the NES panel studies, in particular, the 1992-1994-1996 panel study. I can examine voters who are unsorted[1] in 1992 but who are sorted in 1994 and 1996. I can then compare their behavior in 1992 (when they are unsorted) with their behavior in 1996 (when they are sorted). If my hypotheses are correct, these voters will display higher levels of party loyalty at the ballot box in 1996 than in 1992: sorted voters will be more loyal to their party than unsorted ones.[2]

TABLE 7.1 **Effects of sorting on voting behavior**

Activity	1992 Behavior (%)	1996 Behavior (%)	Difference	χ^2 Statistic	p-Value
Voting for one's same-party nominee	72	97	25	7.3	<0.01
Split-ticket voting	39	23	16	1.3	0.13

Note: The table compares the voting behavior of voters who sort between 1992 and 1994 in 1992 (before sorting) with their behavior in 1996 (after sorting); see the text for additional details.

Because I am comparing the same individuals pre- and postsorting, I can rule out the possibility that my results are being driven by some unmeasured demographic or attitudinal characteristic beyond sorting. My results can therefore be interpreted as the direct effect of sorting on voting behavior.

Table 7.1 gives the results of implementing this pre/post design using the 1992-1994-1996 NES panel data. If my hypotheses are correct, I expect to find that, after sorting (1996), these voters are more likely to support their same-party nominee and less likely to split their ticket than they were before sorting (1992). The data strongly support my hypotheses. The first row of table 7.1 shows how likely voters were to support their same-party presidential nominee before sorting (in 1992) and after sorting (in 1996). In 1992, 72 percent of these individuals voted for their same-party nominee. But in 1996, 97 percent of these individuals supported their same-party nominee, a difference of 25 percent, which is highly statistically significant ($\chi^2 = 7.3$, $p < 0.01$, one-tailed).[3] The same finding holds in the second row, where I examine split-ticket voting. After sorting, 16 percent fewer voters split their tickets (though the difference is only marginally statistically significant). In both analyses, voters are more loyal to their party after sorting than before. Sorting—by removing cross-pressures from a voter's decision calculus—changes voter behavior.[4]

Affect toward the Parties

What about the effects beyond voting? I argue that sorting should also change how voters *feel* about the parties. More specifically, sorted voters should evaluate their own party more positively and the opposing party more negatively. This follows because sorting, by anchoring voters more firmly to their party, heightens the "perceptual screen" induced by partisanship (Campbell et al. 1980), drawing the voters' attention to the positive aspects of their party and to the negative aspects of the other party. Respondents' perceptions of the parties should therefore polarize after sorting: they should like their own party more and the other party less.

To test this hypothesis, I examine voters' evaluations of the parties and candidates using the NES "feeling thermometer" scales. These scales ask respondents to rate how positively or negatively they feel toward the parties and candidates using a temperature-like scale, with positive ("warmer") evaluations being scored more highly. These feeling thermometer ratings allow me to capture (a crude approximation of) respondents' affective judgments about the parties (for a review of the measurement of emotion and affect in politics, see Marcus 2000). If my hypothesis is correct, I expect to find larger differences in respondents' feeling thermometer ratings of the national parties and candidates after sorting (relative to before sorting). Table 7.2 gives the results.

The data strongly support this affective polarization hypothesis. After sorting, voters' affective evaluations of the parties are 19 points more polarized (on a 100-point scale). To give a sense of the magnitude of this difference, note that the warmest average feeling thermometer rating was 70.1 degrees for Robert Kennedy in 1968 just after his assassination, and the lowest was 31.2 degrees for Richard Nixon in 1976 after he had resigned in disgrace (Anderson and Granberg, 1991, 148). Given this compression of the ratings in the middle of the scale, this 19-point difference is all the more impressive. This polarization is due to both liking one's own party more and liking the other party less—after sorting, voters feel 13 degrees warmer toward their own party, and 6 degrees cooler toward the

TABLE 7.2 **Effects of sorting on affective evaluation**

Activity	1992 Rating	1996 Rating	Difference	t Statistic	p-Value
Evaluations of the parties:					
Difference between party evaluations	21	40	19	3.7	< 0.01
Same-party evaluation	62	75	13	5.1	< 0.01
Other-party evaluation	41	35	6	1.7	0.05
Evaluations of Candidates:					
Difference between presidential nominees	18	44	26	3.9	< 0.01
Difference between vice-presidential nominees	16	33	17	3.3	< 0.01

Note: Table follows the same format as table 7.1; see there for additional details.

opposite party.[5] So sorting, by anchoring voters more firmly to one side of the political aisle, draws them emotionally closer to their own party and farther away from the other party.

This same affective polarization also extends to candidate evaluations. In 1992 (presorting), 18 points (on average) separates the two presidential nominees' ratings on the feeling thermometer scale. But after sorting (in 1996), that difference more than doubles to 44 points; a similar pattern holds for the evaluation of the vice-presidential nominees. One obvious limitation of these candidate-based tests is that the nominees change between 1992 and 1996, and so part of this difference may stem from changes in how people see the nominees (e.g., a Republican may simply prefer Bob Dole as a candidate to George H. W. Bush). The enormous differences in ratings, combined with the effect on the party evaluations, however, suggest that sorting plays an independent role as well. These results make it clear that sorting helps to divide up respondents into "teams": once voters are sorted, they view their own party more positively and view the other party more negatively.

Attitude Effects

Sorting may also affect voters' attitudes as well. For example, imagine a Republican voter who is pro-choice and favors increasing taxes. After seeing Republican elites consistently espouse cutting taxes, he too begins to support lower taxes (i.e., he sorts on taxes). Does he then also become pro-life as well? This voter has already learned that conservative Republican elites share his values on one issue (taxes), so it should not be a stretch to imagine that they also share his values on another (abortion). Indeed, this sense of shared values underlies theories of cue taking from elites more generally: I know that Democrats share my beliefs about the role of government, so if I agree with them on one position, it should be easy to imagine that I agree with them on another (Zaller 1992). Thus, sorting should also drive an attitude effect here as well. Once a voter sorts, he should adopt his party's position on a range of other issues.

To explore this possibility, I examined whether or not voters take their party's position on eight issues asked in both the 1992 and 1996 waves of the NES panel data: the government services and spending scale, the guaranteed jobs scale, the defense spending scale, the aid to minorities scale, government health insurance, and the respondent's position on abortion, affirmative action, and laws to prevent job discrimination against homo-

TABLE 7.3 **Effects of sorting on voter attitudes**

Activity	1992 Agreement (%)	1996 Agreement (%)	Difference	χ^2 Statistic	p-Value
Abortion	49	71	22	4.3	0.02
Government services and spending	47	71	24	5.1	0.01
Guaranteed jobs	45	64	19	2.9	0.05
Aid to minorities	29	68	39	13.9	< 0.01
Defense spending	33	47	14	1.5	0.11
Affirmative action	43	74	31	8.6	< 0.01
Government vs. private health insurance	42	61	19	2.5	0.06
Homosexual job discrimination	52	63	11	0.8	0.19

Note: Table follows the same format as table 7.1; see there for additional details.

sexuals.[6] If my hypothesis is correct, then I expect to see more voters take their party's position in 1996 after they become sorted. Table 7.3 gives the results.

For every issue, there is at least an 11-point increase in agreement with one's party after sorting. Respondents are significantly more likely to adopt their party's positions on *other* issues as a result of sorting. So when respondents move from being liberal Republicans to being conservative Republicans, for example; not only does this have implications for their ideological self-identification, but it also has enormous consequences for their views on affirmative action, abortion, and a variety of other issues.[7]

One might ask whether these attitude effects also increase polarization. There is reason to suspect that they might: as voters adopt their party's positions on these issues after sorting, they will (on average) move away from the center of the ideological spectrum and toward the poles (see the discussion in chapter 1). But just as in the case of sorting more generally (see chapter 3), the effect is quite limited. When respondents adjust their attitudes postsorting, they move them only 1–2 scale positions. This type of shift is unlikely to appreciably increase aggregate polarization.

These attitudinal effects do, however, significantly increase voter *consistency,* the tendency of attitudes to fall into predictably liberal or conservative clusters (Nie and Andersen 1974). Table 7.3 demonstrates that sorting itself drives voters to adopt their party's perspective on a host of issues: as I move from being a liberal Republican to being a conservative Republican, I also adjust my views on abortion, tax cuts, etc. So after sorting, voters will hold more consistently liberal/conservative clusters of attitudes than they did before sorting. While prior work has recognized a linkage between sorting and consistency (e.g., Nie and Andersen 1974; Layman and Carsey 2002a), the size of the effects in table 7.3 suggests that this relationship is even more significant than previous work had argued.

Robustness Checks

While these effects are impressive, it may be that I have simply detected a secular trend occurring throughout the electorate and incorrectly attributed it to sorting. So, for example, perhaps party voting is increasing among all voters, not just among the sorted, and table 7.1 simply reflects that pattern. To ensure that this is not the case, I estimated three additional robustness checks. First, I replicated these results (when possible) in the 1972-1974-1976 and 2000-2002-2004 NES panel studies, and the same patterns emerged in all three studies. So if this sort of secular-trend story were true, it would need to be true at all three points in time. Second, I also analyzed the data using a between-subjects test. This test compares two groups of voters: those who move from unsorted to sorted during the panel study (e.g., those who are unsorted in 1992 but are sorted in 1994 and 1996) and those who remain unsorted throughout. If the secular-trend story were true, then there should be no difference between these two groups of voters: the trend should change behavior in both groups in the same way. The results support my story rather than this alternative hypothesis: those who move from unsorted to sorted become much more loyal to their party than those who do not. Finally, I conducted two "placebo" tests: I examined changes in attitudes, behavior, and affect among those who were unsorted in all three periods and among those who were sorted in all periods. Generally speaking, I found no consistent pattern of differences in attitudes, behavior, or affect among these voters, which effectively rules out a secular-trend argument. The results I present here demonstrate that sorting itself, not some other, unmeasured factor, is what changes voters' behavior.

Sorting Voters into Teams

The results above demonstrate that sorting helps make voters more loyal members of their "teams": after sorting, they are more loyal to their party at the ballot box, they are more likely to take their party's positions on the issues, and they evaluate their own party more positively. Together, these changes help to explain a variety of over-time macrodevelopments in American elections. Levels of party voting have surged to near-record-highs over the past few elections (Hetherington 2001; Bartels 2000). Extrapolating from my results above, I find that nearly one-quarter of the increase in party voting observed since the 1970s is due to a replacement of unsorted voters (more cross-pressured and hence less loyal to their party) with sorted voters (with fewer cross-pressures and hence more party loyalty).[8] Prior scholarship correctly identifies polarized elites as the root explanation for these higher levels of party loyalty in the electorate but overlooks the unique contribution of sorting to this process. My analysis therefore more clearly elucidates the causal mechanism driving this increasing party loyalty in the electorate.

My results further imply that the party voting observed today is quite different from the party voting of half a century ago. Given the rise of sorting, today's voters are much more likely to agree with their party on the issues than their compatriots from the Eisenhower era were. This is party voting based not just on socialization and parental party ID but also on a growing agreement with the party on issues, which has important implications for elite behavior that I discuss below.

My results also partially explain the recent trends in polarized evaluations of political figures (e.g., the large differences between Democrats and Republicans in their evaluations of President Bush and other political figures; see Jacobson 2006; Shapiro and Bloch-Elkon 2006). While the polarized *actions* of political elites are certainly a key factor driving this polarization (Fiorina and Levendusky 2006a), my results demonstrate that sorting itself also plays a role. As voters sort, their evaluations of political figures (particularly, salient figures like presidential nominees) polarize. As sorting increases, the baseline level of affective polarization grows, regardless of elite action. This points to a potentially pernicious consequence of sorting: this affective polarization may make it harder for politicians to reach out to voters outside their party, particularly when they are pursuing contentious policies (I return to this point later in the chapter).

A similar pattern also holds for the over-time increase in attitude consistency (Layman and Carsey 2002a; however, see Baldassarri and Gelman 2008). Previous studies have likely *understated* the effect of sorting on attitude consistency. They do so because they miss an important effect of sorting on attitude consistency: when a voter sorts, he moves *other* attitudes into alignment with his party ID. So when a voter sorts on (say) abortion, he also becomes more likely to agree with his party on defense spending as well. Over time, this type of sorting-driven increase in consistency makes the mass parties more ideologically homogeneous.

Overall, these results are clear: sorting, by removing cross-pressures from voters, anchors them more firmly to one side of the political aisle. After sorting, voters are more inclined to support and root for their "team," which has a host of important consequences, which I detail below.

How Sorting Changes Campaigns

These electoral changes have significant consequences for how *candidates* behave. For half a century, the conventional wisdom—among both political scientists and journalists—was that, to win an American election, candidates should focus on appealing to the center to convert the critical "swing" voters.[9] Campaigns focus on swing voters because they expect them to yield a large payoff in votes. They know their own base will turn out for their side, so they need not invest many resources there. Likewise, resources devoted to the opposition's base are wasted: those voters will turn out for their party's candidate. That leaves those without strong ties—the swing voters—as the key to winning elections (Stimson 2004; Mayer 2007; Calmes and Harwood 2004). The Downsian model of elections provides the theoretical underpinnings for this strategy. In Downs's model, the median voter was the pivotal voter, and by definition, the median voter will be someone in the middle, without strong ties to either party: a swing voter (Downs 1957). Given this theoretical result, a swing voter strategy should be an election-winning strategy.

This swing voter strategy also dictated campaigns' resource allocation. Although over-time data on campaign expenditures are scarce, campaign insiders (such as 2004 Bush strategist Matthew Dowd) suggest that the vast majority of campaign funds—around 80 percent—have traditionally been devoted to converting undecided swing voters (Bergan et al. 2005, 762; see also Morton 2006; Edsall 2006a). The parties employed a strategy based on appealing to the center, at least at the presidential level.

But beginning in the 1990s, campaigns began to shift from this swing voter strategy to a base mobilization strategy. Party mobilization efforts have increasingly been focused on ensuring that the party faithful turn out rather than on trying to find and convert likely nonvoters (Goldstein and

Ridout 2002; Fiorina 1999). This base voter strategy reached its apotheosis in 2004, when the parties decided that mobilizing the base, not converting swing voters, was the path to victory. In 2004, the Bush team decided to spend almost half of its budget mobilizing the Republican base, a major shift from previous elections. Indeed, the budget for voter mobilization in 2004 was three times the 2000 election budget for similar efforts (Morton 2006). And likewise, though it received far less media attention, Democratic groups—particularly labor unions and the "527s" like MoveOn.org and America Coming Together—also appealed heavily to liberal voters, minorities, and labor union members. In particular, the Democratic strategy in Ohio (dominated by America Coming Together) was to maximize voter mobilization in densely populated urban areas and Democratic suburbs at the expense of trying to convert undecided voters in other areas (Bai 2004). Judging by the campaigns' focus, the base, not the middle, was the key to victory in 2004. The parties moved from following Downs's 1957 advice to focus on the median voter to Huntington's 1950 advice to mobilize their core supporters.

But why have the parties shifted their focus so dramatically over the past few decades?[10] The two strategies that campaigns use (targeting swing voters or targeting the base) are really the same strategy; the difference between them is the likelihood that the targeted voter turns out to vote for the party (Hillygus and Shields 2008). Nevertheless, the point remains that the parties began to invest more heavily in the base mobilization strategy, although continuing to spend considerable resources courting the swing voters as well. This shift requires an explanation.

Sorting provides a partial answer.[11] Given a changing political environment—the growing size of the political base—the parties adapted by changing their strategy. As the number of sorted voters becomes larger (and the size of the base increases), the relative costs of the base and swing voter strategies shift—base voters become a potentially more lucrative source of votes than swing voters. While not all campaigns adopt this base mobilization strategy, a well-sorted electorate makes this strategy possible.[12]

This sort of shift—more emphasis on the base—also highlights the growing importance of targeting in election campaigns. The messages that motivate core partisans and sorted voters to head to the polls are quite different from the messages that encourage swing voters to step off the fence (Holbrook and McClurg 2005). As a result, the ability of campaigns to target voters has become increasingly important (Hillygus and Monson 2008; Hillygus and Shields 2008; Edsall and Grimaldi 2004). This is not to claim that targeted appeals are aimed at only sorted voters—clearly, they are not (Hillygus and Monson 2008; Hillygus and Shields 2008). However, it does suggest that sorted voters may be a particularly important group receiving these sorts of messages, and that the messages they receive should be quite different from those aimed at swing voters.

Though sorting helps to explain this shift toward the base, this should not be read as an argument that the parties ignore the political center: neither party has a sufficiently large base that they can win by base appeals alone (Bai 2004). Both parties therefore invest considerable resources in courting undecided and cross-pressured partisans. For example, in 2004, both parties spent considerable time discussing the importance of various valence issues, such as providing prescription drugs to seniors, improving education, expanding access to health care, and so on. Campaigns need to construct a coalition from both base and swing voters, so they try to find ways to speak to both groups. To consistently win elections, candidates need to appeal to the center as well as to their base (see also Hillygus and Shields 2008).

One natural question to ask is whether or not this outcome—a balance between base and centrist appeals, with an emphasis on base appeals—is an equilibrium (in the informal sense of the word). Given the current configuration of elites and voters in American politics, it seems unlikely that the system will change absent some sort of exogenous shock to it. The politicians who can best navigate this system are the ones like Bill Clinton who can appeal to the base yet still speak to the center. Although it is hard to remember this in today's partisan environment, this was the strategy George W. Bush pursued in 2000: he campaigned as a "compassionate conservative, a uniter not a divider," and so on. He was a governor who campaigned on his record of bipartisanship and improving education to appeal to the center but also managed to convince the conservative base of his credentials, particularly during the Republican primaries (for a description of Bush's centrist strategy in 2000, see Edsall 2006b). Though more ideologically extreme candidates increase turnout among their base, this polarization decreases turnout among moderates, suggesting that a balance of appeals to the base and to the center is needed to win elections (Peress 2006). This balance—an ability to mobilize the base while also appealing to the center—may be the informal equilibrium in the current political environment.

But this base versus swing voter strategy also has an interesting implication for future scholarship: does the strategy a candidate pursues to win an election affect the policies he can achieve once in office? Anecdotal evidence in Halpern and Harris 2006 certainly suggests so. They argue that a centrist, swing voter strategy (which they label [Bill] "Clinton politics") allows a candidate to achieve fairly high approval ratings, but only if he pursues modest, consensual policies. In contrast, they argue that a base strategy (which they label [George W.] "Bush politics") frees a candidate's hand to pursue a more ideologically pure set of policies (indeed, given the ideological tenor of such a victory, this strategy might require it). They argue that this more ideological approach can result in more sweeping policy changes, though actually enacting these changes may require overcoming opposition from other parts of the political spectrum. This last point may be particularly true in a well-sorted electorate, given the findings on affective polarization reported earlier. If a politician pursues polarizing policies, he will most likely struggle to attract support from partisans of the other party, and therefore maintaining his own base will be crucial. This implies that a politician can pursue polarizing policies only when he has a highly cohesive political base. More systematic research is needed before we can draw these types of conclusions with confidence, but this suggests an exciting opportunity for future scholars to examine how electoral strategies impact governance.

Polarized Elites, Sorted Voters

While elites have polarized quite dramatically since the 1960s (McCarty, Poole, and Rosenthal 2006), ordinary voters have not (see the discussion in chapter 3). The distribution of voters has remained relatively constant while the distribution of elites has shifted quite dramatically. This finding is puzzling in light of the standard results in spatial models of party competition. These models typically predict that, if the distribution of voters changes only a small amount, candidate positions should likewise remain relatively constant (Calvert 1985; McKelvey 1986; Besley and Case 2003). But this prediction is at odds with the empirical reality: voters have changed only a small amount, but elites have become much more ideologically polarized. How can I reconcile the predictions from these models with the observed reality?

One explanation for this disjunction is that these models never really applied to the American case. But this is empirically not true. During the 1950s and 1960s, the parties were remarkable for their high degree of ideological overlap and bipartisanship, at both the mass and elite levels, suggesting that candidates were converging to the median voter (Han and Brady 2007; McCarty, Poole, and Rosenthal 2006). By contrast, today's candidates provide voters much more choice than echo and no longer seem to demonstrate these same centrist tendencies. Although spatial models once explained the American case quite well, they no longer seem to do so.

This division between masses and elites speaks to the very heart of American democracy, suggesting a disconnect between rulers and ruled (Fiorina and Abrams 2009). There are obviously no simple answers to this problem, and a complete resolution is beyond the scope of this project.[13] That said, my findings demonstrate how sorting can help to explain this puzzle.

The empirical results from earlier in this chapter highlight how even a small change in the distribution of voters can have dramatic consequences. Although sorting has only a minor effect on the distribution of opinion (e.g., the increase in polarization has been quite limited), it has a much larger effect on factors like voter consistency. When a voter sorts, he brings his issue positions into alignment with one another—his attitudes become more consistent with one another. As a result, the mass parties become more internally homogeneous. While this process has limits (e.g., it does not create an electorate of sophisticated ideologues), it does make the distribution of opinion within the party more homogeneous.

While the change in the distribution of voters is quite modest, the implications for candidates are much more profound. The increasing voter consistency engendered by sorting should increase the pressure on candidates to take noncentrist positions, particularly at the primary level. Efforts to moderate and move toward the center would leave the politician vulnerable to a potential primary challenge from the fringes (Stimson 2004).[14] In other words, more homogeneous within-party distributions of opinion give candidates incentives to move away from the center either to win a primary election or to avoid a challenge altogether.[15]

The claim I am making here is *not* that sorting or primary elections cause elite polarization. Indeed, elite polarization causes sorting, not the reverse. But while the causal arrow begins with elites, there is an important feedback loop here. Once elite polarization generates voter sorting, the shape of the primary electorate changes and becomes more homogeneous. This more homogeneous primary electorate makes it more challenging for candidates to move toward the ideological center, thereby sustaining elite polarization. While sorting is not the initial cause of elite polarization, it may help to maintain elite polarization once it exists.

These theoretical conclusions are consistent with the empirical data. Primary challenges are rare, but that could well result from candidates acting strategically to avoid them. Nearly all incumbent primary losses happen when an incumbent is "outflanked" by a more extreme challenger, such as Lamont's defeat of Lieberman in the 2006 Connecticut Senate primary (Brady, Han, and Pope 2007).

Further, sorting may intensify the sorts of biases identified by Van Houweling and Sniderman (2006). These authors show experimentally that a powerful partisan bias typically exists when voters evaluate candidates: Democratic voters almost always favor the Democratic candidate over the Republican candidate, even when the Republican's policy is *unambiguously* closer to the voter's preferred policy. I have no direct evidence that sorting increases the biases, but given the evidence presented earlier on the effects of sorting, it is not unreasonable to suggest that sorted voters may display even stronger versions of these partisan biases than other voters. If this is true even to a small extent, candidates may face even less pressure to move back to the political center than they would otherwise. In other words, a better-sorted electorate may not punish candidates very much for moving to the ideological poles.

This represents important progress toward resolving the disconnect between voters and elites. The key insight is that small shifts in the distribution of voter ideology such as sorting can have major implications for candidate behavior. Although sorting has only very slightly increased polarization, it has major consequences for the homogeneity of the mass parties. Even if many voters have remained relatively centrist, they are now much more firmly anchored to their side of the aisle. As a result, candidates do not seem to need to hew as closely to the center as they once did. It is not the size of changes that matters; it is the quality of those changes.[16]

How the Masses Shape Elite Behavior

These results also demonstrate that the mass public constrains elite behavior in important ways. While the causal arrow initially runs from elites to masses, once the mass public begins to sort, those changes can also fundamentally shape elite behavior. Sorting, combined with various institutional arrangements, changes the balance of centrifugal and centripetal forces in elections. As the electorate sorted during the 1980s, 1990s, and 2000s, this shift reinforced rising levels of congressional polarization. Glaeser, Ponzetto, and Shapiro (2005) formalize a similar logic. They develop a model where, in equilibrium, candidates will move toward the ideological poles away from the median voter. Candidates pursue this strategy because moving away from the median voter mobilizes their base and increases their turnout. With a more well sorted electorate, candidates should be more able to take noncentrist issue positions.[17]

The debate over censure versus impeachment for President Clinton nicely illustrates this point. During the Clinton impeachment scandal, the popular press argued that, while individual members of Congress might have favored censure (or a more moderate outcome), the House leadership whipped members into supporting impeachment. An alternative explanation is that members were concerned about a primary challenge: if they appeared too soft on Clinton, they might anger the hard-core conservatives in their district, which could lead to a challenge from a more conservative opponent in the next election (Fiorina 2001). Even if members of Congress might prefer to moderate on policy, the activists prevent them from doing so.

Congressional politics also shifts more broadly as a result of these changes. To the extent that these sorts of electoral changes prevent members from returning to the ideological center, they may reduce the number of moderate legislators over time. The number of moderate legislators—who can reach out across the parties and broker compromise—is an important predictor of the amount of significant legislation passed by the Congress (Binder 1999). So with fewer moderates, it might become harder to structure the compromises needed to pass significant policy reforms. Further, with fewer moderates, there may well be a rise in the sort of partisan bickering and "blame game" politics as the two sides cluster into two disparate camps (Groseclose and McCarty 2001; Gilmour 1995).

Finally, increases in sorting may also have implications for the types of leaders selected by the congressional parties and the types of strategies they choose to pursue. As the mass parties become somewhat more homogeneous, the congressional parties can opt to select stronger leaders with more centralized power (Cooper and Brady 1981). This, in turn, has important implications for the debates over the rise of "strong" congressional parties (Rohde 1991; Cox and McCubbins 1993). While more empirical data will be needed to test these sorts of arguments, they suggest that sorting may have consequences not only for elite polarization but for elite politics more generally.

Primary Elections

The changes to primary electorates brought by sorting can also help to explain recent trends in primary election contestation. In the 2004 and 2006 election cycles, several well-known moderate senators from both parties—Arlen Specter (R-PA), Lincoln Chaffee (R-RI), and Joe Lieberman (D-CT)—faced tough primary election battles. Although Lieberman eventually won the general election running as an independent candidate, he was defeated by political neophyte Ned Lamont in the Democratic primary, the first time an incumbent senator had lost a primary election since Bumpers's defeat of Fulbright in 1974. Typically, senators (and members of the House) attract little competition at the primary level, so why have three prominent senators (one of whom would have been vice president, save for a ballot design error) faced serious primary competition in the last few election cycles?

The results discussed above suggest an answer. Both the growing homogeneity of primary electorates and the potential biases of sorted voters potentially put more moderate candidates at risk. Commenting on the 2006 primary election season, one journalist noted:

> Activists groups were pivotal in both races. In Connecticut, liberal MoveOn .org was at the center of a constellation of anti-war Democrats and blogosphere activists who mounted a murderously effective campaign to paint Lieberman as a sycophant for President Bush. In Michigan, [Seventh District House primary challenger Tim] Walberg got backing from Right to Life Michigan and the Club for Growth, a national anti-tax group that attacks so called RINOs—Republicans in name only—it deems insufficiently conservative.[18] . . . Like the Saudi religious police who roam the streets enforcing Islamic strictures on behavior, party activists increasingly punish those who stray from the approved line. (*USA Today*, 2006)

With more homogeneous primary electorates (and ideological interest groups that target moderate politicians), politicians who are out of line with the primary electorate are increasingly in danger of losing their jobs (Eilperin and Grunwald 2007).[19] Republicans tend to be better sorted than their Democratic counterparts, so one might expect to see somewhat more difficulty for the remaining moderate Republican legislators. However, as the examples here suggest, neither party is immune from these sorts of primary challenges (or threats of challenges) from the purists. Among the committed, moderation and bipartisanship are seen as weaknesses, not virtues. An increasingly well-sorted and homogeneous electorate only makes it more likely that moderate legislators will continue to face electoral competition at the primary level.[20]

Will Sorting Continue?

The above discussion demonstrates that sorting has important effects on American politics. But will sorting (and these effects) continue into the future? At the outset, let me say that this type of speculation can be ill-advised. That said, it appears reasonable to suggest that there is an upper bound on the amount of party sorting that can take place. Today there are fewer regional differences than there were thirty years ago, which provides a functional limit on sorting.

Even more importantly, elite Democrats and Republicans are ideologically unified today in a way that they simply were not a generation ago. Although internal ideological differences are still present (e.g., Olympia Snowe is not Trent Lott, and Jim Webb is not Ted Kennedy), these differences are minor compared with those from a generation ago. Given that the contemporary elite parties are relatively homogeneous, the cues they send to voters are unlikely to become much clearer in the coming years. This will likely slow the pace of sorting.

Further, if sorting continues indefinitely, eventually the only people left who are unsorted will be the chronically inattentive and politically uninformed citizens. These people are unlikely to notice elite cues regardless of their clarity, and so they will almost certainly not sort. The presence of these politically disengaged voters will limit the amount of sorting.

Another alternative is that continued high levels of elite polarization will simply lead some voters to disengage from one or both of the parties (for an elaboration of this idea, see Fiorina, Abrams, and Pope 2005). For example, recently a number of prominent Kansas Republicans left the party over their frustration with its extremity and focus on social issues at the expense of other concerns (Slevin 2006). While it is difficult to know if this is the beginning of a trend or an isolated incident, it does raise the possibility that sharply polarized elites will lead some individuals to either leave their party or (in a more extreme version) leave politics altogether. If moderates are turned off by ideological extremism, they may be unwilling to adopt the stances of either party, which would also limit sorting.

The role of valence issues, as I discussed in chapter 2, also limits sorting. When the parties discuss "honest government" and "real security" at a broad level with few details of specific policy proposals, respondents do not learn what set of policy positions accompanies their party identification. These types of appeals provide another check on sorting.

The parties may also moderate their stances over time, which would limit sorting as well. Both parties have moved to soften their rhetoric on social issues in recent years (Bai 2006; Toner 2007), and there seem to be some efforts at bipartisanship in the wake of Obama's historic win (Harwood 2008). Only time will tell if this is merely empty rhetoric or if this is a new trend among elites to strive for the middle. Whatever one concludes about this specific case, efforts by the parties to moderate their ideological stances and reach across the aisle would also provide a practical limit on sorting. Indeed, if one wanted to reduce the amount of sorting in the mass electorate, the most direct way would be for the elites to moderate their policy positions or offer more heterogeneous cues: have prominent Democrats repeatedly speak out against gun control and for tax cuts, or have leading Republicans explain time and again why abortion rights should be protected. Such moves would almost certainly reduce party sorting over time.

There is one countertrend, however, that might lead to *more* sorting. As I discussed in earlier chapters, the political environment experienced by young adults exerts a powerful influence on their partisan and ideological identifications for the rest of their lives (Green, Palmquist, and Schickler 2002; Stoker and Jennings 2008). There has been a sharp swing back to the Democratic Party among young voters during the Bush administration (Jacobson 2008). New voters entering the electorate during the Bush era have been 15 percent more Democratic than Republican, the largest difference ever recorded (Jacobson 2008). These individuals are also more likely to identify as liberals than their older peers. This raises the possibility of a number of new sorted Democrats entering the electorate. Of course, it is also known that many life events push voters in a more conservative direction (Jennings and Niemi 1981), so it is unclear what the future holds. But it does suggest that the clear policy signals from the parties during the Bush administration did shape the behavior of young voters, potentially with consequences for years to come.

Overall, then, it is more difficult to predict with any accuracy whether or not sorting will continue into the future. Assessing all of these trends together, it seems plausible that, though sorting may continue to increase in the short term, it will eventually either stabilize or decline. Of course, the biggest unknown factor will be the continued behavior of political elites. If they continue to take polarized positions, then sorting will likely continue. If they do not, then that shift could well change the electoral landscape in fairly dramatic ways.

Sorting and Democratic Citizenship

My results make it plain that sorting has important implications for citizens' behavior and attitudes. Sorting anchors voters more firmly to one side of the political spectrum, and as a result, they are much more closely bound to "their" party. These results also illustrate why sorting is *normatively* desirable: sorting ties voters to their party, which in turn allows them to make better decisions. Strong party ties are vital to a healthy democracy: party is the vehicle through which ordinary voters can connect their underlying values to a vote choice (Hetherington 2001, 629). This is the classic Schattschneiderian view of political parties: they are the thread that connects the mass public to government policies (Burnham 1982). Sorting helps voters vote "correctly" by connecting their beliefs to their vote choice (Lau and Redlawsk 1997; Lau, Andersen, and Redlawsk 2008). Sorting, simply put, makes for better citizens. As such, sorting is a "good" thing.

But at the same time, sorting also balkanizes the electorate in potentially harmful ways. The role of sorting in the growth of affective polarization most clearly illustrates this point: after sorting, people's emotional responses to the parties become more polarized. One side is my team, the "good" guys, and the other side is the "bad" guys. This is not to suggest that ordinary Americans are entered into the sort of pitched battle that elites are: they most clearly are not (Fiorina, Abrams, and Pope 2005). But the evidence is clear that there are emotional consequences to sorting that make voters more partisan. Sorting, then, "invites into politics passions that cannot easily be brokered or negotiated" (Muirhead 2006, 715). Viewed in this light, perhaps sorting is not such a good thing after all.

This highlights the fundamental tension inherent in the standards for good citizens discussed by political scientists. On the one hand, we ask people to be active and enthusiastic participants in the democratic process. Yet at the same time, we also argue that citizens should put "principles above party," to think carefully about the issues of the day and not to depend on party to guide their decisions. Discussions of participatory democracy inevitably assume that partisanship will play a minor role. Scholars speak of the "ideal of the Independent citizen," one who is "attentive to politics, concerned with the course of government, who weighs the rival appeal of a campaign and reaches a judgment that is unswayed by partisan prejudice" (Campbell et al. 1980, 143). They assume that "citizens are at their best not when they are partisan, but when they are independent" (Muirhead 2006, 714). Good citizens—the kind we want to encourage—participate, but they set aside their partisan convictions when they do so.

My results show that this is an impossible standard for ordinary citizens to meet in real life. Sorting allows people to participate in a more meaningful way, but it also makes people more partisan. If political scientists think that citizens' meaningful participation (as in "correct" voting or higher levels of attitude consistency) matters, then we may have to overcome our qualms about partisanship—there are not many viable alternative mechanisms for engaging citizens more fully with the political process. If we remove partisanship from politics, then we also remove the desire that inspires people to participate in the first place. When we remove the passion from politics, participation drops (Schudson 1998). After all, it is parties and partisans "who make the political world turn. It is they who, disproportionately, keep informed, show up to vote, and fuel campaigns. They are the ones who cheer in joy and mourn in sorrow on election night—and either way, steel themselves for another fight" (Muirhead 2006, 723; see also more generally the discussion in Rosenblum 2008).

In short, either sorting has improved citizens, or we need new standards for citizenship. If what we want is more people to enthusiastically cheer for their side, and to have some way of translating their underlying preferences into votes, then sorting is unquestionably a positive development. But if so, we should accept that such participation runs a risk of attaching people more tightly to a party and inducing them to view politics in those terms.

The price for more engagement, enthusiasm, and "correct" voting is a heightened partisan spirit in the electorate. We should abandon quixotic standards for ideal citizenship that bear little resemblance to real-world politics (Bartels 2003). If citizens can participate meaningfully only by relying on political parties (Sniderman and Levendusky 2007), then we should decide whether the benefits of such participation are worth the costs.

The Positive Side of Elite Polarization

Sorting also allows us to cast the debate over elite polarization in a new light. Few recent political developments have been as decried as elite polarization: it is seen as a scourge on modern American democracy that threatens the health of our nation (McCarty, Poole, and Rosenthal 2006; Galston and Nivola 2006). The consequences of this polarization are profound and fundamental: it threatens the ability of the Congress to pass laws (Sinclair 2008), the independence of the judiciary (Binder 2008), and the ability of our nation to have a successful foreign policy (Beinart 2008). From this perspective, elite polarization is indeed a negative development.[21]

Yet less attention has been paid to the effects on voters. My results here suggest that whatever else it may generate, elite polarization helps voters to participate more effectively. Divided elites generate voter sorting, which in turn increases "correct" voting and attitude consistency. These electoral implications provide at least a partial counterweight to the litany of negative consequences discussed by other scholars (for another optimistic assessment of the effects of polarization for voters, see Hetherington 2008).

This dustup over the effects of elite polarization highlights a connection to an older debate. For most of the twentieth century, the primary concern of party scholars was *not* that politics was too polarized. Rather, it was that politics was *not polarized enough*. Scholars talked about the decline of parties and the resulting dealignment of the electorate (Wattenberg 1998; Dalton and Wattenberg 2000; Broder 1972). Ideologically heterogeneous elite parties meant that party cues were less relevant to ordinary voters than they had once been, and as a result, voters increasingly saw the parties as irrelevant to American politics (Burnham 1982; Wattenberg 1998; Nie, Verba, and Petrocik 1979). This political malaise was seen as a reflection of a deeper crisis of legitimacy in American society, one that could be cured only by a wholesale change in American politics. Many of these scholars turned to the sorts of arguments suggested by earlier party reformers, most notably the American Political Science Association's Committee on Political Parties. The committee argued that America needed "responsible parties" in the European model: ideologically divided parties that presented voters with a programmatic choice so voters could appropriately reward policy successes and punish policy failures (Committee on Political Parties 1950). Such changes, they argued, would once again render parties relevant for American politics.

But fast-forward a generation, and it becomes clear that, perhaps unintentionally, American parties *did* take some of this advice (Rae 2007). Whatever other weaknesses they might have, the Democrats and the Republicans *do* present clear and vastly different alternatives to the voters on a host of issues, and ordinary citizens do perceive these contrasts between the parties. As the parties became more ideologically divided on the issues of the day, ordinary voters not only perceived this differentiation but also exploited it to align their own party and issue positions. While the more grim predictions of the decline-of-parties literature failed to emerge (e.g., Burnham's 1982 argument that dealignment had generated a "crisis" that could be resolved only with a major change in American society), they *were* correct in some of their assessments of the party system: when the parties divided over key issues and explained to voters how party was relevant to policy, partisanship reemerged with a vengeance in American politics.

This, in turn, highlights once again the tough choices facing not only scholars but ordinary Americans. Elite polarization does seem to have a host of negative consequences. But at the same time, it has a series of positive ones for American voters. So if we move, as Galston and Nivola (2008) suggest, "toward depolarization," then the electoral connection between voters and parties will almost certainly weaken again, as it did in the 1950s and early 1960s. In another generation, we will most likely be decrying "me-tooism" among political elites, much as our intellectual grandfathers did fifty years ago. Whether or not the trade-off between less polarization and a weaker electoral connection is a good one depends upon one's particular values and judgments. But it reminds us that in politics, as in life more generally, there are rarely, if ever, any easy choices.

Appendix

Data Used

This appendix explains the data used throughout this manuscript. I have grouped the data by source rather than by chapter. For the details of where and when each data source was used, please see the body of the text.

The National Election Study

The NES is the long-standing benchmark study of the American public. Here, I used two different sources: the cumulative data file (years 1972–2004) and the 1992-1994-1996 panel study. I describe the items I used from them in turn.

The Cumulative Data File

This section gives the question wordings used in the over-time analysis from the NES. Note that the wordings below are for the self-placement versions of the items. The party placements are identical except voters are asked to place the Democratic and Republican parties on this same scale: "Where would you place The [Republican/Democratic] party on this scale?" See the codebook to Krosnick and Lupia 2005 for more details on the administration of these items.

Party ID: "Generally speaking, do you usually think of yourself as a Republican, a Democrat, an Independent, or what?" (IF REPUBLICAN OR DEMOCRAT:) "Would you call yourself a strong (REP/DEM) or a not very strong (REP/DEM)?" (IF INDEPENDENT, OTHER [1966 AND LATER: OR NO PREFERENCE]:) "Do you think of yourself as closer to the Republican or Democratic party?" The responses to these items are then combined into the standard seven-point partisanship scale running from "strong Democrat" to "strong Republican" (see Campbell et al. 1980 for more details).

Liberal-Conservative Self-Identification: "We hear a lot of talk these days about liberals and conservatives. Here is [1972, 1974: I'm going to show you] a 7-point scale on which the political views that people might hold are arranged from extremely liberal to extremely conservative. Where would you place yourself on this scale, or haven't you thought much about this?" Respondents are then shown a seven-point scale, with all options fully labeled. The points are (1) "Extremely liberal," (2) "Liberal," (3) "Somewhat liberal," (4) "Moderate, middle of the road," (5) "Slightly conservative," (6) "Conservative," (7) "Extremely conservative."

Aid to Minorities: Two very slightly different versions of this item were used. After 1990, respondents were asked: "Some people feel that the government in Washington should make every possible effort to improve the social and economic position of blacks. Others feel that the government should not make any special effort to help blacks because they should help themselves. Where would you place yourself on this scale, or haven't you thought much about it?" Prior to 1988, respondents were asked: "Some people feel that the government in Washington should make every possible effort to improve the social and economic position of blacks and other minority groups [1980: even if it means giving them preferential treatment]. Others feel that the government should not make any special effort to help minorities because they should help themselves." In 1988, both versions were administered to half-samples. Respondents were then asked to select their position on a seven-point scale with point 1 labeled "Government should help blacks/minority groups" and point 7 labeled "Blacks/minority groups should help themselves" and all other points unlabeled.

Abortion: "There has been some discussion about abortion during recent years. (RESPONDENT BOOKLET) Which one of the opinions on this page best agrees with your view? You can just tell me the number of the opinion you choose. (1) By law, abortion should never be permitted. (2) The law should permit abortion only in case of rape, incest, or when the woman's life is in danger. (3) The law should permit abortion for reasons other than rape, incest, or danger to the woman's life, but only after the need for the abortion has been clearly established. (4) By law, a woman should always be able to obtain an abortion as a matter of personal choice."

Government Services/Spending Trade-Off: "Some people think the government should provide fewer services, even in areas such as health and education, in order to reduce spending. [2004: Suppose these people are at one end of a scale, at point 1.] Other people feel that it is important for the government to provide many more services even if it means an increase in spending. [2004: Suppose these people are at the other end, at point 7. And, of course, some other people have opinions somewhere in between, at points 2, 3, 4, 5, or 6.] Where would you place yourself on this scale, or haven't you thought much about this?" Respondents are then shown a seven-point scale with point 1 labeled "Government should provide many fewer services: reduce spending a lot" and point 7 labeled "Government should provide many more services: increase spending a lot" and all other points unlabeled.

Defense Spending: "Some people believe that we should spend much less money for defense. [1996, 2004: Suppose these people are at one end of a scale, at point 1.] Others feel that defense spending should be greatly increased. [1996, 2004: Suppose these people are at the other end, at point 7.] [2004: And, of course, some other people have opinions somewhere in between, at points 2, 3, 4, 5, or 6.] Where would you place yourself on this scale or haven't you thought much about this?" Respondents are then shown a seven-point scale with point 1 labeled "Greatly decrease defense spending" and point 7 labeled "Greatly increase defense spending" and all other points unlabeled.

Government's Role in Guaranteeing Each Citizen a Job: "Some people feel that the government in Washington should see to it that every person has a job and a good standard of living. [1972–1978, 1996–LATER: Suppose these people are at one end of a scale, at point 1.] Others think the government should just let each person get ahead on his/their own. [1972–1978, 1996: Suppose these people are at the other end, at point 7. And, of course, some other people have opinions somewhere in between, at points 2, 3, 4, 5 or 6.] Where would you place yourself on this scale, or haven't you thought much about this?" Respondents are then shown a seven-point scale with point 1 labeled "Government see to job and good standard of living" and point 7 labeled "Government let each person get ahead on his own" and all other points unlabeled.

Government's Role in Providing Citizens with Health Care: "There is much concern about the rapid rise in medical and hospital costs. Some people feel there should be a government insurance plan which would cover all medical and hospital expenses [1994: for everyone]. Others feel that medical expenses should be paid by individuals, and through private insurance [1996: plans] like Blue Cross [1994: or (1996: some) other company paid plans]. Where would you place yourself on this scale, or haven't you thought much about this?" Respondents are then shown a seven-point scale with point 1 labeled "Government insurance plan" and point 7 labeled "Private insurance plan" and all other points unlabeled.

Affirmative Action: "Some people say that because of past discrimination blacks should be given preference in hiring and promotion. Others say that such preference in hiring and promotion of blacks is wrong because it gives blacks advantages they haven't earned. What about your opinion—are you for or against preferential hiring and promotion of blacks?" Respondents are coded for or against these programs. Democrats are sorted on this issue if they support affirmative action programs; Republicans, if they oppose them. For the analysis by region, southerners are those from the eleven states of the former Confederacy.

Income Measures: Using the NES household income scale, I code respondents into the top, middle, and bottom thirds of the income scale. The item reads: "Please look at this page and tell me the letter of the income group that includes the income of all members of your family living here in [year] before taxes. This figure should

include salaries, wages, pensions, dividends, interest, and all other income. (IF UN-
CERTAIN: What would be your best guess?")

Male: Interviewers are asked (after the in-person interview), "Respondent's sex
is: Male or Female?" Males are coded as 1, females as 0.

Race: Interviewers are asked (after the in-person interview), "Respondent's race
is: WHITE, BLACK, AMERICAN INDIAN OR ALASKAN NATIVE, ASIAN OR PACIFIC ISLANDER,
or Other?" Note that an interviewer-assigned code is used for the responses before
2000, and afterward respondents are asked to self-identify using the scale provided.

Political Information (Interviewer Rating Item): After completing the interview,
interviewers are asked to respond to this item: "Respondent's general level of information about politics and public affairs seemed: Very high, Fairly high, Average,
Fairly low, Very low." In the over-time analysis in chapter 4, I reversed the scale
coding so the item runs from low to high.

1992-1994-1996 Panel Data

This describes the items used from the 1992-1994-1996 panel data. Unless otherwise noted, the question wordings used in this study are identical to those reported
for the cumulative data file above.

General Political Information: In the analysis in chapter 4, I use a factual knowledge scale built from a variety of knowledge items. For 1992, I use the interviewer's
assessment of the respondent's level of political information (both pre- and post-
election interviews),[1] whether the respondent can name the position currently held
by various political figures (Dan Quayle, William Rehnquist, Boris Yeltsin, and
Tom Foley),[2] whether or not the respondent knows which branch of government
has the final say in whether or not a law is constitutional,[3] and finally whether or
not the respondent knows who has the responsibility to nominate judges to the
federal courts.[4] For 1994, the items used are the interviewer's assessment of the
respondent's level of political information (both pre- and postelection interviews),
whether the respondent can name the position currently held by various political
figures (Al Gore, William Rehnquist, Boris Yeltsin, and Tom Foley), whether or
not the respondent knows which branch of government has the final say in whether
or not a law is constitutional, whether or not the respondent knows who has the responsibility to nominate judges to the federal courts, and finally whether or not the
respondent knows which party currently controls the House of Representatives.[5]
To make comparisons across years easier, I sum the number of correct answers and
normalize the measure (so the mean of the measure is 0 and a 1 unit change is a 1
standard deviation change).

Gay Antidiscrimination Laws: "Do you favor or oppose laws to protect homo-
sexuals against job discrimination?"

Presidential Vote: If respondents report having voted for a candidate for president in the November general election, they are asked, "Who did you vote for?"
and are then given the names of the candidates.

Split-Ticket Voting: Following standard conventions in the literature (Kimball 2004), I define a "split-ticket" vote as selecting a candidate from one party at the presidential level but a candidate from the other party at the House level (e.g., supporting the Democratic nominee for president but voting for a Republican House candidate). The House vote choice question directly parallels the presidential vote question given above.

Feeling Thermometers: Respondents are asked: "Now looking at page 2 of the booklet, I'd like to get your feelings toward some of our political leaders and other people who are in the news these days. I'll read the name of a person and I'd like you to rate that person using something we call the feeling thermometer.

"Ratings between 50 degrees and 100 degrees mean that you feel favorable and warm toward the person. Ratings between 0 degrees and 50 degrees mean that you don't feel favorable toward the person and that you don't care too much for that person.

"You would rate the person at the 50 degree mark if you don't feel particularly warm or cold toward the person. If we come to a person whose name you don't recognize, you don't need to rate that person. Just tell me and we'll move on to the next one."

These data, reported in the text, come from evaluations of "The Democratic Party, "The Republican Party," "liberals," and "conservatives" on this scale.

General Social Survey Data

The General Social Survey (GSS) is another long-standing study of the attitudes of the American public. The GSS provided me with the data for the analysis of the role of fundamentalism in the abortion debate in chapter 3.

Abortion Index: Respondents were asked a series of six yes/no questions about the circumstances under which they would permit abortion. Before each item, respondents were asked, "Please tell me whether or not you think it should be possible for a pregnant woman to obtain a legal abortion," and then they were read the specific circumstances: "If she is married and does not want any more children?" "If there is a strong chance of serious defect in the baby?" "If the family has a very low income and cannot afford any more children?" "If she is not married and does not want to marry the man?" "If the woman's own health is seriously endangered by the pregnancy?" and "If she became pregnant as a result of rape?" The index used in the text is a scale ranging from zero to six giving the number of circumstances in which the respondent would permit legal abortion.

Fundamentalist: Respondents were asked: "What is your religious preference? Is it Protestant, Catholic, Jewish, some other religion, or no religion?" For those who are Protestant, the GSS asks about their specific church and, on that basis, codes individuals according to a three-part scheme: "Fundamentalist," "Moderate," "Liberal." The coding is based upon the beliefs of particular denominations.

Here, I treat those coded as "Fundamentalist" by the GSS as actually being fundamentalist (given a value of 1 for this variable); others are coded as 0. For details on
the GSS coding rules, see "GSS Methodological Report 43."[6]

Stem Cell Data

This section gives the question wording for the stem cell data. See the detailed discussion at the Roper Center Archives for more details (www.ropercenter.uconn.edu).

Stem Cell Opinions: In 2001, respondents were asked: "Sometimes fertility
clinics produce extra fertilized eggs, also called embryos, that are not implanted
in a woman's womb. These extra embryos either are discarded or couples can
donate them for use in medical research called stem-cell research. Some people
(support stem-cell research, saying it's an important way to find treatments for
many diseases). Other people (oppose stem-cell research, saying it's wrong to use
any human embryos for research purposes). What about you—do you support
or oppose stem-cell research?" Note that the items in parentheses were rotated
across respondents. Respondents could then either support or oppose stem cell
research. In 2005, respondents were asked: "Do you support or oppose embryonic
(EMBRY-onick) stem cell research?" Again, respondents were presented with a
binary response option (support/oppose). So the difference between the two years
was that in 2001 respondents were given a brief introduction to stem cell research,
unlike in 2005.

Party ID: Respondents were asked: "Generally speaking, do you usually think
of yourself as: a Democrat, a Republican, an Independent, or what?" Those who
initially claimed to be independents were then asked: "Do you lean more toward the
Democratic Party or Republican Party?" This results in a five-point party ID scale
(Democrat, leaning Democrat, Independent, leaning Republican, Republican).

Liberal-Conservative Self-Identification: "Would you say your views on most political matters are liberal, moderate, or conservative?" This results in a three-point
scale (liberal/moderate/conservative).

College Graduate: "What was the last grade of school you completed? (1) 8th
grade or less, (2) Some high school, (3) Graduated high school, (4) Some college
(ASK IF TECHNICAL SCHOOL; IF YES, PUNCH CODE 3, FOR HIGH SCHOOL), (5) Graduated
College, (6) Post-graduate." Those who completed college or had postgraduate
studies are coded as 1; all others, 0.

Respondent's Age: "What is your age?" Responses are given in years. Note that
in the results in table 5.1 I divided age by 10 to aid in coefficient interpretation.

Evangelical: "Would you consider yourself a born-again or evangelical Christian, or not?" Those who respond yes are coded as 1; all others, 0.

Catholic: "What, if anything, is your religion?" Those who respond that they are
Catholic are coded as 1; all others, 0.

Income: 2001 item: "If you added together the yearly incomes, before taxes, of all the members of your household for the last year, 2000, would the total be (followed by a list)?" In 2005, respondents were asked: "Which of the following CATEGORIES best describes your total annual household income before taxes, from all sources?" Slightly different scales were used in the two years. To aid in comparability, I used a four-point scale: (1) less than $20,000, (2) $20,000–$50,000, (3) $50,000–$75,000, and (4) more than $75,000. Differences between the scales in the two years prevent more fine-grained analysis of income.

Original Experimental Data

This section gives the question wording for the original experiments (embedded within the Knowledge Networks survey) used in chapter 5. See Levendusky 2008 for more details.

Specific-Attitude Items

Before respondents read about each issue, they were read the following text.

(IF MODERATE ELITES OR POLARIZED ELITES CONDITION:) "Please read about each issue and study the positions of the two parties. After you've had a chance to study the positions of the parties, then move on to the next screen to register your own opinion on each issue. For each policy, we will tell you where members of Congress from both parties stand. The data comes from a scientific study conducted by the Congressional Research Center for the official Congressional Record. The opinions of Democrats are shown with blue stick-people and Republicans are shown with red stick-people. Each symbol you see on the screen symbolizes 25 members of Congress, so the more symbols by a position, the more members of Congress agree with a position."

(IF CONTROL:) "Please read about each issue and then use the scale to tell us what you think about this issue."

Army Corps of Engineers: The U.S. Army Corps of Engineers is a federal government agency that develops the nation's waterways. For example, the Corps helps to design most of the nation's dams and flood control projects. Recently, some have argued that more independent review of Corps projects by outside engineers is needed to protect environmentally sensitive areas. Critics disagree, and argue that these reviews add unnecessary costs and slow down development too much.

How about you? Do you agree or disagree that more independent review of Corps projects is needed?

Strongly agree[7]
Somewhat agree

Neither agree nor disagree
Somewhat disagree
Strongly disagree

Air Traffic Controllers: Air traffic controllers are currently employees of the U.S. government. Some people have proposed allowing private firms, rather than the federal government, to be in charge of air traffic controllers.

How about you? Do you agree or disagree with allowing private companies to control air traffic controllers?

Coastal Drilling: Drilling for oil and natural gas is currently prohibited along most areas of the U.S. coastline. Some people have proposed eliminating this restriction, which would result in more exploration for oil and natural gas along the U.S. coast.

How about you? Do you agree or disagree with maintaining the ban on coastal drilling?

Job-Training Programs: The federal government currently has the primary responsibility for developing and carrying out many types of job-training programs. Some people have argued that the federal government should instead allow state governments to have primary control over these job-training programs.

How about you? Do you agree or disagree with giving state governments primary control over job-training programs?

Electricity Deregulation: The rates power companies charge consumers for electricity are currently regulated by state and federal laws. Some people want to eliminate these laws and allow market forces to set the price of electricity.

How about you? Do you agree or disagree with eliminating government regulation of electricity rates?

Manipulation Check Items

After expressing their attitudes on these five policy items, subjects were asked the following item, designed to assess their perceptions of the degree of elite polarization.

"On (NAME OF ISSUE), do Democrats and Republicans in Congress take very similar views on this issue, somewhat similar views, somewhat different views, or very different views?"

Very similar views
Somewhat similar views
Somewhat different views
Very different views

Notes

Chapter One

1. On the ideological heterogeneity of the parties in the 1960s and 1970s, see Campbell et al. 1980; Mclosky, Hoffmann, and O'Hara 1960. On party voting and split-ticket voting, see Bartels 2000. On voter dealignment, see Burnham 1982; Wattenberg 1998. On the contemporary resurgence of party, see Abramowitz and Saunders 1998; Hetherington 2001. On President Obama as "postpartisan," see Budowsky 2008. Data on the level of party voting comes from the National Exit Polls, as reported by CNN (see http://www.cnn.com/ELECTION/2008/results/polls). On elite polarization, see Theriault 2008; McCarty, Poole, and Rosenthal 2006.

2. This may raise the question of *why* elites have polarized. This is a distinct question from my focus here: I take it as a matter of empirical regularity that elites have moved, and I proceed from that basis. For a review of the formal theoretic literature explaining why elites move, see Grofman 2004. For the relevant empirical literature, see the summaries in Theriault 2008; Han and Brady 2007; Sinclair 2006. In particular, the hypothesis that changing patterns of interest group participation generated political polarization deserves more investigation. In the late 1960s and early 1970s, interest groups began to become involved in politics in new ways, which changed the composition of the activists of both parties, and also recruited a new type of more issue-driven candidate (Brady, Han, and Pope 2007; Layman 2001). More work, however, remains to be done on this point before this can be shown to be a key cause of elite polarization.

3. Fiorina (2002) was the first to use the term "sorting" in this context.

4. This is what Fiorina, Abrams, and Pope (2005) call "popular polarization." I use the simpler "polarization" throughout the text.

5. Note that my definition of "polarization" excludes some of what scholars term "polarization" in the literature. In particular, it does not encompass discussions of geographic segregation into liberal or conservative areas (Bishop 2008),

the tendency toward polarized evaluations (e.g., Democrats and Republicans differing sharply in their evaluations of President Bush; see Jacobson 2006; Shapiro and Bloch-Elkon 2006), or the idea that polarization is synonymous with ideological consistency/constraint (Abramowitz 2007; though see Hetherington 2009). For a broader overview of the various components of the polarization debate, see Fiorina and Abrams 2008; Hetherington 2009; Galston and Nivola 2006.

6. That said, if the reader prefers the term "partisan polarization" for some reason, it can be substituted for "sorting" in the text without any change in meaning.

7. The reader may wonder whether or not it is possible to have a polarized electorate that is not sorted. It is possible, but arguably not politically interesting: this would be a scenario where all respondents have passionate extreme views about an issue, but that issue does not map onto the political divide (i.e., Democrats and Republicans are equally divided between the two camps). Such issues are exceedingly rare: if they existed, then strategic elites would attempt to exploit them to build a new winning coalition (see Schattschneider 1960).

8. The argument is *not* that the mass public blindly follows wherever elites lead. Rather, it is simply that most changes of this sort begin at the elite level and filter down to the mass public (see, e.g., Carmines and Stimson 1989). For more on this point, see the discussion in chapter 2.

9. I say "partially" because other key factors have also contributed to the growth of this strategy, most notably the media environment (Prior 2007) and campaign technology (Hillygus and Shields 2008). Although sorting is a key part of the story, it is not the whole story.

10. To be clear, the claim is not that sorting forces parties to adopt a base strategy. Rather, it is that sorting *permits* the parties to adopt this strategy if they so choose.

11. While not all scholars view elite polarization in a negative light (e.g., Sinclair 2006), it is fair to say that the conventional wisdom is that elite polarization is a negative development.

12. All the key results are given in the text. For some analyses, however, certain readers may be interested in robustness checks (using different variables, coding rules, and so forth). I have made many of these results available in an online appendix at http://www.press.uchicago.edu/books/levendusky. The interested reader is urged to consult that appendix for additional details.

Chapter Two

1. The idea of party reputation (or party labels) is not simply theoretical: real-world politicians think in the same terms. Representative John Carter (R-TX), commenting on the Republican Party in 2006, argued that "we're [the Repub-

lican Party] trying to . . . define ourselves. What are Republicans?" (Weisman 2007)

2. Technically, elite polarization need not make the parties more internally homogeneous, but it almost always does so for the reasons discussed below.

3. One concern here is that "issue ownership" might lead to both sides simply emphasizing different sets of issues, with no overlap. But recent research suggests that this is not the case: candidates engage in dialogue. If your opponent brings up issue X, you must respond to that issue, even if it is "owned" by the other party (Siegelman and Buell 2004; Kaplan, Park, and Ridout 2006).

4. A related possibility is that the growing amounts of money in politics (from both interest groups and individuals) allow the parties more opportunities to define their positions more clearly (by, say, allowing them to sponsor more issue advertisements). A full consideration of this hypothesis would require parsing out what parties actually do with this money, and hence is beyond the scope of this project. It does, however, provide an intriguing possibility for future research.

5. Another factor that may affect sorting is politicians' use of "crafted talk," where they use public opinion not to decide what policies they should pursue but rather to decide how to frame their policy appeals (Jacobs and Shapiro 2000). This could potentially cut either way, however: politicians might prime people to think about certain issues by using crafted talk, but they might do so in a less polarizing way. Ultimately, the relationship between crafted talk and the clarity of the parties' positions is unclear.

6. Over time, candidates' advertisements have become more important, and the news itself less important, as a source for policy information (Gilens, Vavreck, and Cohen 2007). This may also increase the ease with which voters receive partisan cues.

7. Many of these narrowcast programs also feature what Mutz calls "in your face" television: programs that violate conversational norms by shouting and emphasizing conflict rather than rational, civilized debate. Her research shows that people come to see the opposition as less legitimate after watching these programs (Mutz and Reeves 2005; Mutz 2007). This tendency should only further accentuate the attachment to one's own side of the political aisle, which may further accelerate sorting.

8. The data that do exist for activists—the Convention Delegate Studies—suggest that activists have polarized on the issues in much the same way as elites have; see Sinclair 2006 for more details.

9. The full text of the acceptance speeches and the party platforms both come from the American Presidency Project; see Woolley and Peters 2005 for more details.

10. Although I do not report it here in the interest of space, I have also used Poole and Rosenthal's 1997 NOMINATE scores to measure party positions over time. The conclusions from the NOMINATE-based analysis are similar to the ones

I report here: the elite parties are increasingly farther apart ideologically and more internally homogeneous.

11. George McGovern, acceptance speech, 1972 Democratic Convention, Miami, FL. The text of the speech comes from Woolley and Peters 2005.

12. As quoted in Layman 2001, 10.

13. Of course, with these new socially conservative voters as part of the base, that changes the calculation of elites. Although elites were originally responsible for bringing social issues (and hence religious evangelical voters) into the mix, once there, the behavior of ordinary voters would then constrain elite behavior.

14. Ronald Reagan, remarks accepting the presidential nomination, Dallas, TX. Text of the speech comes from Woolley and Peters 2005.

15. Clinton, Jackman, and Rivers (2004) estimate that John Kerry, based on his voting record in the 107th Congress, was in the most liberal quintile of the U.S. Senate. Likewise, they estimate that George W. Bush (based on his announced positions) would be in the most conservative quintile.

16. To show the mutability of these positions, contrast George W. Bush in 2000 versus George W. Bush in 2004 on the use of the military.

17. There are two general types of issues relevant to politics: positional issues and valence issues. Positional issues are issues like abortion or defense spending where the parties take sides (pro-life vs. pro-choice, more money for defense vs. less, etc.). A valence issue, by contrast, is one where everyone agrees on the goal in question, like honesty, fighting corruption, safety, etc.

18. Author's personal communication with Democratic National Committee staff, January 2007.

19. Information about The Democratic Vision can be downloaded from the Democratic National Committee's homepage at http://www.democrats.org/agenda. html, accessed 3 January 2007.

20. The search begins in 1980 because that is when Lexis-Nexis coverage of the *Times* begins. I utilized the Proquest Historical Newspaper Archive to do a search of the *Times* during the 1970s. Doing so indicated very few stories about polarization during that period. I opted to use Lexis-Nexis (rather than Proquest) for the 1980–2004 period given the vastly superior search tools of Lexis-Nexis.

21. There is another aspect to the media coverage of polarization as well: the increasing focus on conflictual reporting (Cappella and Jamieson 1997; Patterson 1994). Some argue that elite polarization drives this sort of coverage (Jacobs 1998). This type of coverage may also make it increasingly clear to the public that elites take divergent positions, though I leave a more careful examination of this hypothesis for future work.

22. I take it to be a different argument that elites changed because a different set of activists became involved with the primary process, either at the presidential level (Layman 2001) or at the congressional level (Brady, Han, and Pope 2007). Party activists should not be taken to hold views reflective of the broader mass public.

Chapter Three

1. For more information on the NES, see http://www.electionstudies.org.

2. As a robustness check, I have examined several other indicators of the clarity of party positions: a measure of "issue clarity" (Carmines and Stimson 1986), the percentage who can correctly place the Democrats to the left of the scale midpoint and the Republicans to the right of the scale midpoint, the percentage who think the Republicans are the more conservative party, and the percentage who perceive there to be "important differences" between the parties. All of these other measures support the finding discussed below, so I omit them here in the interest of space. These supplemental results are available in the online appendix, available at http://www.press.uchicago.edu/books/levendusky.

3. Further, at an absolute minimum, my measure gets at a precondition for sorting in response to elite-driven change. If voters do not recognize that the cues from the parties are now more distinct, then why would they sort? Sorting should be concentrated among those who understand that the parties' positions have become clearer.

4. As is the case almost everywhere in this book, the analysis here begins in 1972, since that is the first year in which many of these questions were asked. The lone exception is the liberal-conservative scale, for which my analysis begins in 1984 since the administration of that item changed then (for the details, see the codebook to Krosnick and Lupia 2005). Including the 1972–1984 data for that item would not change the overall pattern. Additionally, note that, when a question is asked in consecutive years, the points are connected by a line in the figures. When there is a gap in the administration of an item, the points are not connected by a line.

5. Note that figure 3.1 powerfully rebuts the arguments that the parties are simply controlled by a power elite and there is no difference between them (Domhoff 2002). Not only are the parties now farther apart than they were before (see chapter 2), but the mass public also perceives these differences.

6. As a validity check, I examined the extent to which these perception-based measures correlate with actual party positions derived from NOMINATE data. While the relationship is not perfect, it is strong enough to suggest that these changes in voters' perceptions do in fact reflect real changes in elite behavior; these supplemental results are available in the online appendix.

7. From a Bayesian point of view, as people have stronger prior beliefs about the parties' positions, it takes increasingly stronger evidence to change their beliefs.

8. Functionally, on the NES policy scales, this implies that a sorted Democrat takes a position to the left of the midpoint, and a sorted Republican takes a position to the right.

9. The reader may wonder why I did not include the abortion scale in figure 3.1, given its importance to American politics. Unfortunately, the NES has not asked respondents to place the parties on this scale over time.

10. Another possibility to measure sorting would be to calculate the correlation between issue positions and partisanship over time. This approach is potentially problematic, however, given that different items have different formats, and hence different reliabilities and correlations with partisanship over time (Krosnick and Berent 1993). Ultimately, doing the analysis this way would yield similar results (Jacobson 2000).

11. The pattern of sorting varies by party, with more sorted Republicans than sorted Democrats, with the difference undoubtedly stemming at least in part from the different valence of the ideological labels "liberal" and "conservative." I leave exploring these partisan differences for future work.

12. Another topic for future work is why we do not see more sorting early in the time series, especially in light of the divisive policies of the Reagan era.

13. For a similar analysis of sorting at the level of policy agendas, see Fiorina and Levendusky 2006b.

14. Throughout this chapter, I restrict my analysis of racial issues to white respondents only (since if sorting exists on these issues, I expect it to be concentrated among white voters). I have also reestimated sorting on all issues by examining only white voters and find that the substantive conclusions do not change.

15. The figure comes from original survey data that I collected.

16. The data are from a *Los Angeles Times*/Bloomberg Poll conducted 5–9 April 2007, accessed via *National Journal*'s Poll Track, 30 May 2007.

17. In this figure, I collapse respondents into two thirty-year birth cohorts. I do so in the interest of simplicity: analysis with four fifteen-year cohorts did not change the substantive results.

18. For more information on the GSS, see http://www.norc.org/projects/gensoc.asp.

19. The GSS was first conducted in 1972, so the analysis begins in that year.

20. I have also broken down the Democratic data by whether or not the respondent is secular or not (where secular respondents are those who do not claim a religious affiliation or do not attend religious services). A similar (though weaker) pattern also appears in those data, suggesting a parallel process in both parties.

21. Here, I provide only a very brief review of the main findings of the polarization literature. For more detailed overviews of this large literature, see Fiorina and Abrams 2008; Layman, Carsey, and Horowitz 2006; Hetherington 2009.

22. To produce figure 3.7, I recoded the responses to each item into a seven-point scale that ran from most liberal (1) to most conservative (7). Abortion attitudes (measured using a four-point scale) were recoded using the following rule: respondents who would allow abortion as "a matter of personal choice" were coded at 1, those who support abortion when there is a demonstration of a "clear need" were coded at 3, those who support abortion in cases of rape, incest, or life of the mother were coded at 5, and those who feel abortion "should never be permitted"

were coded at 7. Using these recoded scales, I then computed the respondent's average position across all items.

23. Although I disagree with his assertion that sorting and polarization are the same phenomenon (see the discussion in chapter 1), Abramowitz (2006) makes a similar point about sorting being a source of increased polarization.

Chapter Four

1. For more on the measurement properties of this item, see Zaller 1986, 1992. While there are serious limitations to this measure, it is one of the only measures used repeatedly over time by the NES. Therefore, to have comparability over time, it is quite difficult to use any other measure.

2. For a more general discussion of this sort of graphic depiction of regression coefficients, see Gelman and Hill 2007.

3. Though I do not include it here, I can include an interaction term between South and Democrat to test for differences in sorting between northern and southern Democrats. The respecified model reveals only occasional differences, suggesting this regional difference does not play a major role in explaining sorting.

4. Even without the elite placements, the correlation between general political information and my measure of elite polarization is 0.58.

5. Here, I include a lagged dependent variable because it improves the model fit. I have also estimated a more complex statistical model to control for this temporal dependence—a Markov Transition Model (Jackman 2000; Diggle, Liang, and Zeger 2000). The results are the same whether I use the simpler model or the more elaborate MTM. Given this, and the fact that the MTM asks significantly more of the data, I opted for the more direct model described in the text. I also note that the substantive results replicate when the lagged dependent variable is omitted from the model.

6. I have also estimated the effect of two different operationalizations of the elite polarization hypothesis. First, I wanted to explore whether respondents were more sensitive to elite polarization on some issues than on others (e.g., whether sorting is more a product of recognizing elite polarization on, say, abortion than on government spending). To test this alternative hypothesis, I used the respondent's placement of the parties on the issue-specific scales on a variety of economic and social issues. In general, respondents were responsive to elite polarization on both dimensions, but the available measures differed by year, and the conclusions one could draw about the relative sizes of the effects were somewhat sensitive to the specific issues used. Additionally, this is a case where issue importance may be relevant. Those who consider an issue highly important are more likely to be attuned to elite positions on the issue (Krosnick and Petty 1995), and changes in these elite positions should lead to changes in partisanship or other attitudes. Unfortunately,

none of the NES panels have the necessary data on issue importance and perceptions of elites to test this alternative hypothesis.

Second, I also considered the possibility that citizens respond, not to the relative
positions of the parties per se, but rather to the ideological position of *their* party.
I examined whether respondents could successfully place their own party and the
other party on the correct side of the midpoint on the left-right scale. Here, the
results were more ambiguous, due in large part to the fact that most respondents
either know how to place both parties or neither party. Given these limitations, I
present the results using the left-right, liberal-conservative scale and simply note
that these other measures suggest at least a roughly similar substantive conclusion
about the effect of elite polarization on sorting.

7. There is also another possibility here: some people may reverse the meaning
of the labels "liberal" and "conservative" and argue that Democrats are the more
conservative party. These respondents may then, in turn, select the ideological label
they incorrectly *think* matches their national party. So, for example, a respondent
may think Democrats are the conservative party and then call himself a conservative, thinking he has selected the label that matches his party. To test for this effect,
I examined whether those respondents who incorrectly ordered the parties in 1992
then "reverse-sorted" themselves based on this incorrect perception in 1994. Of
those who reversed the ordering of the parties in 1992 but were not reverse-sorted,
16 percent were then reverse-sorted using the incorrect perceptions in 1994, compared to only 6 percent of the remainder of the sample (the difference is statistically
significant using a difference of proportions test). In other words, respondents do
seem to act on these sorts of erroneous beliefs. But two caveats are in order. First,
only 10 percent of respondents reversed the ordering of the parties in 1992, and
second, these respondents were much less politically informed than the remainder
of the sample. Additionally, when contrasting this group with those who correctly
placed the parties and sorted in the model above, one finds that there is more sorting in the "correct" case than in this reverse case, suggesting that the relationship I
discuss in the model above is the stronger, more significant one. In the end, this is an
interesting example of the effect of political perceptions of elites (and their role in
explaining the alignment of party identification and ideological identification), but
the sample is small enough that it may not be particularly politically consequential.

8. To investigate cohort effects more carefully, I have also estimated an age-
period-cohort model. The substantive results reinforce those presented here; see
the online appendix for more details.

Chapter Five

1. The discussion below concerns embryonic stem cells (stem cells extracted
from a several-day-old human embryo) rather than adult stem cells (stem cells

found in mature tissue). For an overview of the distinction and more background on stem cell research, see the briefing materials prepared by the National Institutes of Health (2005).

2. I am deeply indebted to Charles Franklin for bringing the data used in this section to my attention and for providing me with access to his analysis of these data, originally reported in Franklin 2006. It goes without saying that I am solely responsible for any errors in this analysis.

3. For more background on the stem cell controversy, see Nisbet 2004.

4. These studies come from the archives maintained by the Roper Center for Public Opinion Research. They are study number USABCWASH2001-17383 (2001 data) and study number USABCWASH2005-983 (2005 data). See the Roper Center archives for more details (www.ropercenter.uconn.edu).

5. Both studies also ask about support for stem cell research funding. Although I do not report the results here in the interest of parsimony, my primary substantive findings replicate for the support of funding as well.

6. Given this, as one might expect, abortion attitudes tend to be fairly strongly related to attitudes about embryonic stem cell research. I cannot control for abortion attitudes in the analysis presented in this section because questions on abortion are not asked in those surveys. However, an SRBI/*Time* Poll conducted in October 2004 asked about attitudes on abortion and whether or not the respondent supported embryonic stem cell research (see Roper Center study number USSRBI2004-3333 for more details). The attitudes correlate at 0.60, suggesting a strong (though far from perfect) relationship between opposition to abortion and opposition to stem cell research. Although the SRBI/*Time* Poll asks about abortion attitudes, it too suffers from data limitations: it does not ask questions about religious denomination or liberal-conservative ideology. Given these limitations, I present the results from the *Washington Post*/ABC News Poll in the text. However, I have also estimated a model of support for stem cell research using the SRBI data to control for abortion attitudes (though not religion or liberal-conservative views). The primary finding—that the effect of partisanship is larger in the post-2004 study—replicates in this analysis as well.

7. I have also estimated the results omitting the liberal-conservative self-identification measure. The primary substantive result—that the effect of party identification in 2005 is larger than the effect in 2001—remains in this analysis as well.

8. I am deeply indebted to the Institute for the Study of Citizens and Politics at the Annenberg Public Policy Center (and its director, Diana Mutz) for generously funding the survey experiments described in this section. I alone, however, am responsible for any errors of design, interpretation, or judgment in the analyses that follow.

9. As a randomization check, a joint test of statistical significance reveals treatment assignment is not predictable based on background demographic characteristics, ideology, and partisanship ($\chi^2_{25} = 19$, $p = 0.78$).

10. There is a parallel here to Mutz's 2005 study of the effect of social trust. She wanted to understand the consequences of higher/lower levels of social trust for behavior, so she manipulated trust using a doctored story from *Reader's Digest*. The key issue was *not* whether the article changed levels of trust in the real world but whether it changed it in the *experiment*. As long as it changed trust in the experiment, Mutz could use her experimental results to talk about the effect of social trust on behavior. Here, the same argument holds for my experiment: my manipulations do not have to parallel the real-world cues to be valuable; they simply have to change subjects' perceptions of elite polarization.

11. Alternatively, my experiments could also simulate a situation where there is a large elite reshuffling on an issue and citizens need to relearn how party maps onto positions on the issue.

12. Given their similarity in behavior to partisans (Keith et al. 1992), I include partisan leaners in my sample.

13. These results are robust to omitting either the issue fixed effects or the subject random effects (or both).

Chapter Six

1. For an excellent overview of the literature reviewed in this chapter, see Carsey and Layman 2006.

2. To be fair, the possibility that issue positions can change party ID is acknowledged by the authors of *The American Voter:* "if this pressure [from having issue positions out of step with one's party ID] is intense enough, a stable partisan identification may actually be changed" (Campbell et al. 1980, 135).

3. In this analysis, I look at sorting based on changes in level rather than changes in strength. For example, if a respondent moves from being a moderate leaning Democrat to a liberal weak Democrat, that is sorting due to changing ideology.

4. I also broke voters down by age to check for the possibility of cohort effects (e.g., some cohorts, where ideology was more salient, would be more likely to sort by changing their party ID). Unfortunately, the sample sizes are too small to confidently detect whether or not these effects exist.

5. The exception to this pattern of party-driven change is among those who regard an issue as being particularly personally relevant. Carsey and Layman (2006) find that, among these individuals, partisanship is more likely to bend to issue positions rather than the reverse.

6. By branching, I mean that the NES firsts ask whether the respondent is a Democrat, Republican, or independent and then asks about the strength of their identification in a separate question. For more details on branching versus other question formats, see Krosnick and Berent 1993.

Chapter Seven

1. In this analysis, when I say "sorting," I mean this as a shorthand for sorting on the liberal-conservative scale.

2. I look at voters who are sorted in 1994 and 1996 because it allows me to make a cleaner inference about the effects of sorting on behavior. Suppose I only required voters to be sorted in 1996 and compared their 1992 and 1996 behavior. Then I would not know if voters were voting for their party because they were sorted or if the decision to vote for their party in 1996 made them sort. By requiring voters to also be sorted in 1994, I know that sorting temporally precedes the decision to vote Democratic in 1996, thereby allowing me to circumvent this endogeneity.

3. All p-values reported in this chapter are one-tailed, which is appropriate given the directional nature of the hypotheses being tested.

4. As a robustness check, I have rerun these analyses using McNemar's test for paired data (Agresti and Finlay 1997). Using this test does not change the substantive results.

5. A similar result of polarized evaluations of the parties can be obtained by looking at the pattern of likes and dislikes toward the parties; these supplemental results are available in the online appendix.

6. Here, taking the position of one's party is operationalized as it is elsewhere in the text: Democrats take their party's position if they are to the left of the scale midpoint; Republicans take their party's position if they are to the right.

7. There is one limitation to the findings discussed in table 7.3, however. It may be the case that these sorts of effects occur only for issues that are not particularly important to a voter. For highly important issues, voters may *not* change their positions so easily (Krosnick and Petty 1995). Unfortunately, I lack the data needed to test this hypothesis, so I cannot rule out this possibility (for some evidence on this point, see Carsey and Layman 2006). But even if the effect I found occurs only on unimportant issues, it remains a significant finding.

8. The other major change is that even unsorted voters have become more loyal to their parties over time.

9. While each author has his or her own definition of this concept, a "swing voter" is essentially an undecided voter. For more details on this point, see Mayer 2007, 2008.

10. I wish to make clear that my argument is intended to apply only to the past half century or so of political history. In earlier eras, mass-elite interactions were quite different than they are today (Geer 1991): for example, this is the period of the mass-media campaign (Patterson 1994), and there was (possibly) another party system in place prior to the 1960s (Campbell 2006a). Given the fairly dramatic differences between the current period and earlier eras, it is not obvious that my results apply to the scope of American political history. That said, my results *can*

serve as a benchmark for other scholars, though more work will be needed to see if these same patterns hold in earlier eras.

11. I say "partial" because sorting is not the only factor that has changed: for example, campaign technology has also radically transformed (Hillygus and Shields 2008), as has the media environment (Prior 2007).

12. Further, a base mobilization strategy may also be more effective if these individuals are more likely to be embedded in social networks with other sympathetic partisans. If mobilizing base voters has a spillover effect that attracts more voters, then a base mobilization strategy may be particularly efficient (Ensley 2008). More research is needed to empirically verify this, however.

13. For example, a complete resolution of this puzzle requires understanding why American politics became *less* polarized during the 1950s; for more details, see Ansolabehere, Snyder, and Stewart 2001; Han and Brady 2007. My results can only speak to the changes over the past half century.

14. Technically, changes to the voter distribution that do not change the location of the median voter leave the Downsian median voter results intact (Bernhardt, Krasa, and Polborn 2008). But one could imagine an alternative model in which candidates respond (for example) to the shape of their partisan distribution, and therefore a change in the distribution would matter; see Butler 2006 for such a model.

15. I want to avoid pushing too hard on this point, however. Despite its intuitive appeal, the empirical support for this hypothesis is quite mixed (Hirano et al. 2008).

16. As Fiorina and Levendusky (2006b) argue, it is also entirely possible that today's candidates are more ideologically extreme than those of yesteryear—more likely to be recruited from the National Abortion Rights Action League (NARAL) or the National Rifle Association (NRA) than from the Kiwanis Club. Obtaining the data needed to test this hypothesis systematically, however, is nearly impossible. Brady, Han, and Pope (2007) do offer some suggestive evidence in support of this idea, but more remains to be done.

17. For a similar formal logic, see the models of activist politics developed by Miller and Schofield (2003), Aldrich (1995), and Moon (2004). Masket (2007) uses data from a natural experiment in California to demonstrate empirically the logic behind these models: namely, that significant pressure for candidates to polarize comes from relatively extreme party activists and interest groups.

18. The Michigan House primary mentioned here is equally interesting, even if it attracted less attention. First-term incumbent Joe Schwarz, a moderate Republican who supported abortion rights and stem cell research, was defeated by conservative challenger Tim Walberg. Given the smaller size and more homogeneous nature of House districts, the importance of being in line with one's primary constituency is likely even greater than at the senatorial level.

19. A related effect is the death in both parties of Reagan's "11th commandment" (thou shall not speak ill of a fellow Republican).

20. Another possible implication is that sorting will increase members' electoral safety (i.e., increase the incumbency effect). The most obvious mechanism for this sort of an effect would be for sorting to generate more ideologically homogeneous districts, not just more homogeneous parties. There is no direct evidence of this sort of an effect, but it does present an interesting possibility for future research.

21. While not all scholars view elite polarization in a totally negative light (Abramowitz and Saunders 2005), it is fair to say that the conventional wisdom is that elite polarization is a negative development.

Appendix

1. The item reads: "Respondent's general level of information about politics and public affairs seemed: VERY HIGH, FAIRLY HIGH, AVERAGE, FAIRLY LOW, VERY LOW." I recoded the scale so that it runs from low to high.

2. The item reads: "Now we have a set of questions concerning various public figures. We want to see how much information about them gets out to the public from television, newspapers and the like. The first name is XXXX. What job or political office does he now hold?"

3. The item reads: "Who has the final responsibility to decide if a law is constitutional or not: is it the president, the Congress, the Supreme Court, or don't you know?"

4. The item reads: "And whose responsibility is it to nominate judges to the Federal Courts: the president, the Congress, the Supreme Court, or don't you know?"

5. The item reads: "Do you happen to know which party had the most members in the House of Representatives in Washington before the election (this/last) month? (IF NECESSARY: Which one?)"

6. The report is available online at http://webapp.icpsr.umich.edu/GSS/rnd1998/reports/m-reports/meth43.htm.

7. Although I do not repeat them for subsequent items, respondents were shown the same response options for all items.

Bibliography

Abramowitz, Alan. 1994. "Issue Evolution Reconsidered: Racial Attitudes and Partisanship in the U.S. Electorate." *American Journal of Political Science* 38 (1): 1–24.

———. 2006. "Disconnected, or Joined at the Hip? Comment." In *Red and Blue Nation? Characteristics and Causes of America's Polarized Politics*, vol. 1, edited by Pietro Nivola and David Brady. Washington, DC: Brookings Institution Press; Stanford, CA: Hoover Institution.

———. 2007. "Constraint, Ideology, and Polarization in the American Electorate: Evidence from the 2006 Cooperative Congressional Election Study." Paper presented at the annual meeting of the American Political Science Association, Chicago, IL.

Abramowitz, Alan, and Kyle Saunders. 1998. "Ideological Realignment in the U.S. Electorate." *Journal of Politics* 60 (3): 634–652.

———. 2005. "Why Can't We All Just Get Along? The Reality of a Polarized America." *Forum* 3. Available online at http://www.bepress.com/forum.

———. 2008. "Is Polarization a Myth?" *Journal of Politics* 70 (2): 542–555.

Achen, Christopher. 2000. "Warren Miller and the Future of Political Data Analysis." *Political Analysis* 8 (2): 142–146.

———. 2002. "Toward a New Political Methodology: Microfoundations and ART." *Annual Review of Political Science* 5 (1): 423–450.

Achen, Christopher, and Larry Bartels. 2006. "It Feels Like We're Thinking: The Rationalizing Voter and Electoral Democracy." Paper presented at the annual meeting of the American Political Science Association, Philadelphia, PA.

Adams, Greg. 1997. "Abortion: Evidence of Issue Evolution." *American Journal of Political Science* 41 (3): 718–737.

Agresti, Alan, and Barbara Finlay. 1997. *Statistical Methods for the Social Sciences*. 3rd ed. Upper Saddle River, NJ: Prentice Hall.

Aldrich, John. 1995. *Why Parties*? Chicago: University of Chicago Press.

American Association for the Advancement of Science. 2004. "AAAS Policy Brief: Stem Cell Research." Available online at http://www.aaas.org/spp/cstc/briefs/stemcells/index.shtml#decision.

Anderson, Eric, and Donald Granberg. 1991. "Types of Affective Evaluator in Recent U.S. Presidential Elections." *Polity* 24 (1): 147–155.

Ansolabehere, Stephen, Jonathan Rodden, and James Snyder. 2008. "The Strength of Issues: Using Multiple Measures to Gauge Preference Stability, Ideological Constraint, and Issue Voting." *American Political Science Review* 102 (2): 215–232.

Ansolabehere, Stephen, James Snyder, and Charles Stewart. 2001. "Candidate Positioning in U.S. House Elections." *American Journal of Political Science* 45 (1): 136–159.

Baer, Kenneth. 2000. *Reinventing Democrats: The Politics of Liberalism from Reagan to Clinton*. Lawrence: University Press of Kansas.

Bai, Matt. 2004. "Who Lost Ohio?" *New York Times Sunday Magazine*, 21 November.

———. 2006. "The Last 20th-Century Election?" *New York Times*, 19 November.

Baker, Wayne. 2005. *America's Crisis of Values*. Princeton, NJ: Princeton University Press.

Baldassarri, Delia, and Andrew Gelman. 2008. "Partisans without Constraint: Political Polarization and Trends in American Public Opinion." *American Journal of Sociology* 114 (2): 408–446.

Balz, Dan. 2007. "Candidates Still Take Cues from Their Base." *Washington Post*, April 16, A1.

Barnes, Samuel, Max Kaase, Klaus Allerbeck, Barbara Farah, Felix Heunks, Ronald Ingelhart, M. Kent Jennings, Hans Klingemann, Alan Marsh, and Leopold Rosenmayr. 1979. *Political Action: Mass Participation in Five Western Democracies*. Beverly Hills, CA: Sage Publications.

Bartels, Larry. 1993. "Messages Received: The Political Impact of Media Exposure." *American Political Science Review* 87 (2): 267–285.

———. 1996. "Uninformed Votes: Information Effects in Presidential Elections." *American Journal of Political Science* 40 (1): 194–230.

———. 2000. "Partisanship and Voting Behavior, 1952–1996." *American Journal of Political Science* 44 (1): 35–50.

———. 2002. "Beyond the Running Tally: Partisan Bias in Political Perceptions." *Political Behavior* 24 (2): 117–150.

———. 2003. "Democracy with Attitudes." In *Electoral Democracy*, edited by Michael B. MacKuen and George Rabinowitz. Ann Arbor: University of Michigan Press.

Baum, Matthew. 2005. *Soft News Goes to War: Public Opinion and American Foreign Policy in the New Media Age*. Princeton, NJ: Princeton University Press.

Baumer, Donald, and Howard Gold. 2007. "Party Images and Partisan Resurgence." *Social Science Journal* 44 (3): 465–479.

Baumgartner, Frank, Suzanna De Boef, and Amber Boydstun. 2008. *The Decline of the Death Penalty and the Discovery of Innocence*. New York: Cambridge University Press.

Beinart, Peter. 2008. "When Politics No Longer Stops at the Water's Edge: Partisan Polarization and Foreign Policy." In *Red and Blue Nation? Consequences and Corrections of America's Polarized Politics*, vol. 2, edited by Pietro Nivola and David Brady. Washington, DC: Brookings Institution Press; Stanford, CA: Hoover Institution.

Bennett, W. Lance. 1990. "Toward a Theory of Press-State Relations in the United States." *Journal of Communication* 40 (2): 103–127.

Berelson, Bernard, Paul Lazarsfeld, and William McPhee. 1954. *Voting: A Study of Opinion Formation in a Presidential Campaign*. Chicago: University of Chicago Press.

Bergan, Daniel, Alan Gerber, Donald Green, and Costas Panagopoulos. 2005. "Grassroots Mobilization and Voter Turnout in 2004." *Public Opinion Quarterly* 60 (5): 760–777.

Bernhardt, Dan, Stefan Krasa, and Mattias Polborn. 2008. "Political Polarization and the Electoral Effects of Media Bias." *Journal of Public Economics* 92 (5–6): 1092–1104.

Berry, Jeffrey. 1984. *The Interest Group Society*. Boston, MA: Little and Brown.

Besley, Timothy, and Anne Case. 2003. "Political Institutions and Policy Choices: Evidence from the United States." *Journal of Economic Literature* 41 (1): 7–73.

Binder, Sarah. 1999. "The Dynamics of Legislative Gridlock, 1947–96." *American Political Science Review* 93 (3): 519–533.

———. 2008. "Consequences for the Courts: Polarized Politics and the Judicial Branch." In *Red and Blue Nation? Consequences and Corrections of America's Polarized Politics*, vol. 2, edited by Pietro Nivola and David Brady. Washington, DC: Brookings Institution Press; Stanford, CA: Hoover Institution.

Bishop, Bill. 2008. *The Big Sort: Why the Clustering of Like-Minded America Is Tearing Us Apart*. New York: Houghton Mifflin.

Black, Earl, and Merle Black. 2002. *The Rise of Southern Republicans*. Cambridge, MA: Harvard University Press.

Brady, David, John Cogan, Brian Gaines, and Douglas Rivers. 1996. "The Perils of Presidential Support: How the Republicans Took the House in the 1994 Midterm Elections." *Political Behavior* 18 (4): 345–367.

Brady, David, Hahrie Han, and Jeremy Pope. 2007. "Primary Elections and Candidate Ideology: Out of Step with the Primary Electorate?" *Legislative Studies Quarterly* 32 (1): 79–105.

Broder, David. 1972. *The Party's Over: The Failure of Politics in America*. New York: Harper and Row.

Brody, Richard. 1991. *Assessing the President*. Stanford, CA: Stanford University Press.

Brody, Richard, and Lawrence Rothenberg. 1988. "The Instability of Partisanship: An Analysis of the 1980 Presidential Election." *British Journal of Political Science* 18 (4): 445–465.

Budowsky, Brent. 2008. "The Post-partisan Realignment." *The Hill (Online Edition)*, 21 October. Available online at http://thehill.com.

Bullock, John. 2006. "Party Cues and Policy Information: Real and Perceived Effects." Manuscript. Stanford University.

Burnham, Walter Dean. 1982. *The Current Crisis in American Politics*. New York: Oxford University Press.

Bush, George W. 2001. "President Discusses Stem Cell Research." 9 August. Available online at http://www.whitehouse.gov.

Butler, Daniel. 2006. "The Electoral Sources of Polarization in the U.S. Congress." PhD dissertation, Stanford University.

Calmes, Jackie, and John Harwood. 2004. "Bush's Big Priority: Energize Conservative Christian Base." *Wall Street Journal*, 30 August, A1.

Calvert, Randall. 1985. "Robustness of the Multidimensional Voting Model: Candidate Motivations, Uncertainty, and Convergence." *American Journal of Political Science* 29 (1): 69–95.

Campbell, Angus, Philip Converse, Warren Miller, and Donald Stokes. 1980. *The American Voter*. Chicago: University of Chicago Press, Midway Reprints.

Campbell, James. 2006a. "Party Systems and Realignments in the United States, 1868–2004." *Social Science History* 30 (3): 359–386.

———. 2006b. "Polarization Runs Deep, Even by Yesterday's Standards—Comment." In *Red and Blue Nation? Characteristics and Causes of America's Polarized Politics*, vol. 1, edited by Pietro Nivola and David Brady. Washington, DC: Brookings Institution Press; Stanford, CA: Hoover Institution.

Cappella, Joseph, and Kathleen Hall Jamieson. 1997. *Spiral of Cynicism: The Press and the Public Good*. New York: Oxford University Press.

Carmines, Edward, and Michael Ensley. 2004. "Policy Preferences and Split-Ticket Voting in the United States." Paper presented at the annual meeting of the American Political Science Association, Chicago, IL.

Carmines, Edward, Jessica Gerrity, and Michael Wagner. 2005. "How Parties Alter Their Reputations on Losing Issues: The Case of the Democrats and Crime." Paper presented at the annual meeting of the Midwest Political Science Association, Chicago, IL.

Carmines, Edward, and James Stimson. 1980. "The Two Faces of Issue Voting." *American Political Science Review* 74 (1): 78–91.

———. 1986. "On the Structure and Sequence of Issue Evolution." *American Political Science Review* 80 (3): 901–920.

———. 1989. *Issue Evolution*. Princeton, NJ: Princeton University Press.

Carsey, Thomas, and Geoffrey Layman. 2006. "Changing Sides or Changing Minds? Party Identification and Policy Preferences in the American Electorate." *American Journal of Political Science* 50 (2): 464–477.

Chen, Anthony, Robert Mickey, and Robert Van Houweling. 2008. "Explaining the Contemporary Alignment of Race and Party: Evidence from California's 1946 Ballot Initiative on Fair Employment." *Studies in American Political Development* 22 (2): 204–228.

Clark, John, John Bruce, John Kessel, and William Jacoby. 1991. "I'd Rather Switch Than Fight: Lifelong Democrats and Converts to Republicanism among Campaign Activists." *American Journal of Political Science* 35 (3): 577–597.

Clinton, Joshua. 2006. "Representation in Congress: Constituents and Roll Calls in the 106th House." *Journal of Politics* 68 (2): 397–409.

Clinton, Joshua, Simon Jackman, and Douglas Rivers. 2004. "The Most Liberal Senator? Analyzing and Interpreting Congressional Roll Calls." *PS: Political Science and Politics* 37 (4): 805–811.

Cohen, Geoffrey. 2003. "Party over Policy: The Dominating Impact of Group Influence on Political Beliefs." *Journal of Personality and Social Psychology* 85 (5):
808–822.

Cohen, Marty, David Karol, Hans Noel, and John Zaller. 2008. *The Party Decides:
Presidential Nominations before and after Reform*. Chicago: University of Chicago Press.

Committee on Political Parties, American Political Science Association. 1950.
"Toward a More Responsible Two-Party System: A Report of the Committee
on Political Parties." *American Political Science Review* 44 (2, Supplement):
1–96.

Connolly, Ceci. 2001. "Legislations See Opening on Stem Cells." *Washington Post*,
17 July, A04.

Conover, Pamela, and Stanley Feldman. 1981. "The Origins and Meaning of Lib-
eral/Conservative Self-Identifications." *American Journal of Political Science*
25 (4): 617–645.

Converse, Philip. 1964. "The Nature of Belief Systems in Mass Publics." In *Ideology and Discontent*, edited by David Apter. New York: Free Press.

———. 2000. "Assessing the Capacity of Mass Electorates." *Annual Review of
Political Science* 3 (1): 331–353.

Cooper, Joseph, and David Brady. 1981. "Institutional Context and Leadership
Style: The House from Cannon to Rayburn." *American Political Science Review*
75 (2): 411–425.

Cowden, Jonathan. 2001. "Southernization of the Nation and Nationalization of
the South: Racial Conservatism, Social Welfare, and White Partisans in the
United States, 1956–92." *British Journal of Political Science* 31 (2): 277–301.

Cox, Gary, and Mathew McCubbins. 1993. *Legislative Leviathan*. Berkeley and Los
Angeles: University of California Press.

Crespino, Joseph. 2007. *In Search of Another Country: Mississippi and the Conservative Counterrevolution*. Princeton, NJ: Princeton University Press.

Dalton, Russell, and Martin Wattenberg. 2000. *Parties without Partisans*. Oxford,
UK: Oxford University Press.

Dawson, Michael. 1994. *Behind the Mule: Race and Class in African-American Politics*. Princeton, NJ: Princeton University Press.

Delli-Carpini, Michael, and Scott Keeter. 1996. *What Americans Know about Politics and Why It Matters*. New Haven, CT: Yale University Press.

Diggle, Peter, Kung-Yee Liang, and Scott Zeger. 2000. *Analysis of Longitudinal
Data*. Oxford, UK: Oxford University Press.

DiMaggio, Paul, John Evans, and Bethany Bryson. 1996. "Have Americans' Social
Attitudes Become More Polarized?" *American Journal of Sociology* 102 (3):
690–755.

Domhoff, G. William. 2002. *Who Rules America?* 4th ed. Boston, MA: McGraw
Hill.

Downs, Anthony. 1957. *An Economic Theory of Democracy*. New York: Harper
and Row.

Druckman, James, and Dennis Chong. 2009. "Identifying Frames in Political News."
In *Sourcebook for Political Communication Research: Methods, Measures*,

and Analytical Techniques, edited by Erik Bucy and R. Lance Holbert. New York: Routledge.

Druckman, James, Lawrence Jacobs, and Eric Ostermeier. 2004. "Candidate Strategies to Prime Issues and Image." *Journal of Politics* 66 (4): 1180–1202.

Edsall, Thomas. 2006a. *Building Red America: The New Conservative Coalition and the Drive for Permanent Power*. New York: Basic Books.

———. 2006b. "Karl Rove's Juggernaut: Party Hardy." *New Republic*, 25 September, 26–29.

Edsall, Thomas, and James Grimaldi. 2004. "On Nov. 2, GOP Got More Bang for Its Billion, Analysis Shows." *Washington Post*, 30 December, A01.

Eilperin, Juliet, and Michael Grunwald. 2007. "The Woman in the Middle: Moderate Democrat Is New Target of Liberal Bloggers." *Washington Post*, 21 February, A01.

Elving, Ronald D. 1988. "Party Platforms Helped Shape Fall Campaigns." *CQ Weekly Report*, 22 October.

Ensley, Michael. 2008. "Candidate Positioning, Ideological Heterogeneity, and Mobilization in U.S. House Elections." Manuscript. Indiana University.

Evans, John. 2003. "Have Americans' Attitudes Become More Polarized? An Update." *Social Science Quarterly* 84 (1): 71–90.

Feinstein, Brian, and Eric Schickler. 2008. "Platforms and Partners: The Civil Rights Realignment Reconsidered." *Studies in American Political Development* 22 (1): 1–31.

Fiorina, Morris. 1981. *Retrospective Voting in American National Elections*. New Haven, CT: Yale University Press.

———. 1999. "Whatever Happened to the Median Voter? Manuscript. Stanford University.

———. 2001. "Keystone Reconsidered." In *Congress Reconsidered*, edited by Lawrence Dodd and Bruce Oppenheimer. 8th ed. Washington, DC: CQ Press.

———. 2002. "Parties and Partisanship: A 40-Year Retrospective." *Political Behavior* 24 (2): 93–115.

Fiorina, Morris, and Samuel Abrams. 2008. "Political Polarization in the American Public." *Annual Review of Political Science* 11 (1): 563–588.

———. 2009. *Disconnect: The Breakdown of Representation in Contemporary America*. Norman: University of Oklahoma Press.

Fiorina, Morris, Samuel Abrams, and Jeremy Pope. 2003. "The 2000 US Presidential Election: Can Retrospective Voting Be Saved? *British Journal of Political Science* 33 (1): 163–187.

———. 2005. *Culture War? The Myth of a Polarized America*. New York: Person Longman.

Fiorina, Morris, and Matthew Levendusky. 2006a. "Disconnected, or Joined at the Hip?—Rejoinder." In *Red and Blue Nation? Characteristics and Causes of America's Polarized Politics*, vol. 1, edited by Pietro Nivola and David Brady. Washington, DC: Brookings Institution Press; Stanford, CA: Hoover Institution.

———. 2006b. "Disconnected: The Political Class versus the People." In *Red and Blue Nation? Characteristics and Causes of America's Polarized Politics*, vol. 1, edited by Pietro Nivola and David Brady. Washington, DC: Brookings Institution Press; Stanford, CA: Hoover Institution.

Franklin, Charles. 1984. "Issue Preferences, Socialization, and the Evolution of Party Identification." *American Journal of Political Science* 28 (3): 459–478.

———. 2006. "Public Support for Stem Cell Research." 19 July. Available online at http://politicalarithmetik.blogspot.com/2006/07/public-support-for-stem-cell-research.html

Franklin, Charles, and John Jackson. 1983. "The Dynamics of Partisan Identification." *American Political Science Review* 77 (4): 957–973.

Franz, Michael, Paul Freedman, Kenneth Goldstein, and Travis Ridout. 2007. *Campaign Advertising and American Democracy*. Philadelphia, PA: Temple University Press.

Freedman, David. 2005. *Statistical Models: Theory and Practice*. New York: Cambridge University Press.

Freire, André. 2008. "Party Polarization and Citizens' Left-Right Orientations." *Party Politics* 14 (2): 189–209.

Fuchs, Dieter, and Hans-Dieter Klingemann. 1990. "The Left-Right Schema." In *Continuities in Political Action: A Longitudinal Study of Political Orientations in Three Western Democracies*, edited by M. Kent Jennings, Jan van Deth, Samuel Barnes, Dieter Fuchs, Felix Heunks, Ronald Ingelhart, Max Kaase, Hans-Dieter Klingemann, and Jacques Thomassen. Berlin: Walter de Gruyter.

Gabel, Matthew, and Kenneth Scheve. 2007. "Mixed Messages: Party Dissent and Mass Opinion on European Integration." *European Union Politics* 8 (1): 37–59.

Galston, William, and Pietro Nivola. 2006. "Delineating the Problem." In *Red and Blue Nation? Characteristics and Causes of America's Polarized Politics*, vol. 1, edited by Pietro Nivola and David Brady. Washington, DC: Brookings Institution Press; Stanford, CA: Hoover Institution.

———. 2008. "Toward Depolarization." In *Red and Blue Nation? Consequences and Corrections of America's Polarized Politics*, vol. 2, edited by Pietro Nivola and David Brady. Washington, DC: Brookings Institution Press; Stanford, CA: Hoover Institution.

Gans, Herbert. 2004. *Deciding What's News*. Evanston, IL: Northwestern University Press.

Geer, John. 1991. "Critical Realignments and the Public Opinion Poll." *Journal of Politics* 53 (2): 434–453.

Gelman, Andrew, and Jennifer Hill. 2007. *Data Analysis Using Regression and Multilevel/Hierarchical Models*. New York: Cambridge University Press.

Gerber, Alan, and Donald Green. 1998. "Rational Learning and Partisan Attitudes." *American Journal of Political Science* 42 (3): 794–818.

———. 1999. "Misperceptions about Perceptual Bias." *Annual Review of Political Science* 2 (1): 189–210.

Gerber, Elisabeth, and John Jackson. 1993. "Endogenous Preferences and the Study of Institutions." *American Political Science Review* 87 (3): 639–656.

Gerring, John. 1997. "Ideology: A Definitional Analysis." *Political Research Quarterly* 50 (4): 957–994.

————. 1998. *Party Ideologies in America, 1828–1996*. New York: Cambridge University Press.

Gerrity, Jessica, Michael Wagner, and Edward Carmines. 2004. "The New Polarization in American Politics: Interest Groups, Mass Media, and Contestation of the Abortion Issue." Paper presented at the annual meeting of the American Political Science Association, Chicago, IL.

Gilens, Martin. 1999. *Why Americans Hate Welfare*. Chicago: University of Chicago Press.

Gilens, Martin, Lynn Vavreck, and Martin Cohen. 2007. "The Mass Media and the Public's Assessments of Presidential Candidates, 1952–2000." *Journal of Politics* 69 (4): 1160–1175.

Gilmour, John. 1995. *Strategic Disagreement: Stalemate in American Politics*. Pittsburgh, PA: University of Pittsburgh Press.

Glaeser, Edward, Giacomo A. M. Ponzetto, and Jessee Shapiro. 2005. "Strategic Extremism: Why Republicans and Democrats Divide on Religious Values." *Quarterly Journal of Economics* 120 (4): 1283–1330.

Goldstein, Kenneth, and Travis Ridout. 2002. "The Politics of Participation: Mobilization and Turnout over Time." *Politial Behavior* 24 (1): 3–29.

Goren, Paul. 2005. "Party Identification and Core Political Values." *American Journal of Political Science* 49 (4): 881–896.

Goren, Paul, and Logan Delancey. 2008. "Party Identification, Issue Attitudes, and the Dynamics of Political Debate." Paper presented at the annual meeting of the American Political Science Association, Boston, MA.

Green, Donald, Bradley Palmquist, and Eric Schickler. 2002. *Partisan Hearts and Minds: Political Parties and the Social Identities of Voters*. New Haven, CT: Yale University Press.

Green, John. 1995. "The Christian Right and the 1994 Elections: A View from the States." *PS: Political Science and Politics* 28 (1): 5–8.

Grofman, Bernard. 2004. "Downs and Two-Party Convergence." *Annual Review of Political Science* 7 (1): 25–46.

Groseclose, Tim, and Nolan McCarty. 2001. "The Politics of Blame: Bargaining before an Audience." *American Journal of Political Science* 45 (1): 100–119.

Hallin, Daniel. 1984. "The Media, the War in Vietnam, and Political Support: A Critique of the Thesis of an Oppositional Media." *Journal of Politics* 46 (1): 2–24.

Halpern, Mark, and John Harris. 2006. *The Way to Win: Taking the White House in 2008*. New York: Random House Books.

Hamilton, James. 2003. *All the News That's Fit to Sell: How the Market Transforms Information into News*. Princeton, NJ: Princeton University Press.

Han, Hahrie, and David Brady. 2007. "A Delayed Return to Historical Norms: Congressional Party Polarization after the Second World War." *British Journal of Political Science* 37 (3): 505–531.

Harwood, John. 2008. "'Partisan' Seeks a Prefix: Bi- or Post-." *New York Times*, 7 December.

Hetherington, Marc. 2001. "Resurgent Mass Partisanship: The Role of Elite Polarization." *American Political Science Review* 95 (3): 619–631.

————. 2008. "Turned Off or Turned On? How Polarization Affects Political Engagement." In *Red and Blue Nation? Consequences and Corrections of America's Polarized Politics*, vol. 2, edited by Pietro Nivola and David Brady. Washington, DC: Brookings Institution Press; Stanford, CA: Hoover Institution.

————. 2009. "Putting Polarization in Perspective." *British Journal of Political Science* 39 (2): 413–448.

Hillygus, D. Sunshine, and Quinn Monson. 2008. "Campaign Microtargeting and Presidential Voting." Paper presented at the annual meeting of the American Association for Public Opinion Research, New Orleans, LA.

Hillygus, D. Sunshine, and Todd Shields. 2008. *The Persuadable Voter: Strategic Candidates and Wedge Issues in Presidential Campaigns*. Princeton, NJ: Princeton University Press.

Hinich, Melvin, and Michael Munger. 1997. *Analytical Politics*. New York: Cambridge University Press.

Hirano, Shigeo, James Snyder, Stephen Ansolabehere, and John Mark Hansen. 2008. "Primary Competition and Partisan Polarization in the U.S. Senate." Manuscript. Columbia University.

Holbrook, Thomas, and Scott McClurg. 2005. "The Mobilization of Core Supporters: Campaigns, Turnout, and Electoral Composition in United States Presidential Elections." *American Journal of Political Science* 49 (4): 689–703.

Huber, Gregory, and John Lapinski. 2006. "The 'Race Card' Revisited: Assessing Racial Priming in Policy Contests." *American Journal of Political Science* 50 (2): 421–440.

Huntington, Samuel. 1950. "A Revised Theory of American Political Parties." *American Political Science Review* 44 (3): 669–677.

Iyengar, Shanto, and Kyu Hahn. 2007. "Red Media, Blue Media: Evidence of Ideological Polarization in Media Use." Paper presented at the annual meeting of the International Comunication Association, San Francisco, CA.

Iyengar, Shanto, Kyu Hahn, Jon Krosnick, and John Walker. 2008. "Selective Exposure to Campaign Communication: The Role of Anticipated Agreement and Issue Public Membership." *Journal of Politics* 70 (1): 186–200.

Jackman, Simon. 2000. "In and Out of War and Peace: Transitional Models of International Conflict." Manuscript. Stanford University.

Jackman, Simon, and D. Sunshine Hillygus. 2003. "Voter Decision Making in Election 2000: Campaign Effects, Partisan Activation and the Clinton Legacy." *American Journal of Political Science* 47 (4): 583–596.

Jacobs, Lawrence. 1998. *Review of Spiral of Cynicism: The Press and the Public Good*, by Joseph Cappella and Kathleen Hall Jamieson. *Public Opinion Quarterly* 62 (2): 282–284.

Jacobs, Lawrence, and Robert Shapiro. 2000. *Politicians Don't Pander: Political Manipulation and the Loss of Democratic Responsiveness*. Chicago: University of Chicago Press.

Jacobson, Gary. 2000. "Party Polarization in National Politics: The Electoral Connection." In *Polarized Politics*, edited by Jon Bond and Richard Fleischner. Washington, DC: Congressional Quarterly Press.

———. 2006. *A Divider, Not a Uniter: George W. Bush and the American People.* New York: Pearson Longman.

———. 2008. "The Effects of the George W. Bush Presidency on Partisan Attitudes." Paper presented at the annual meeting of the Midwest Political Science Association, Chicago, IL.

Jacoby, William. 1988. "The Impact of Party Identification on Issue Attitudes." *American Journal of Political Science* 32 (3): 643–661.

———. 1995. "The Structure of Ideological Thinking in the American Electorate." *American Journal of Political Science* 39 (2): 314–335.

Jennings, M. Kent, and Richard Niemi. 1981. *Generations and Politics: A Panel Study of Young Adults and Their Parents.* Princeton, NJ: Princeton University Press.

Kaplan, Noah, David Park, and Travis Ridout. 2006. "Dialogue in American Political Campaigns? An Examination of Issue Engagement in Candidate Television Advertising." *American Journal of Political Science* 50 (3): 724–736.

Keith, Bruce, David Magleby, Candice Nelson, Elizabeth Orr, Mark Westlye, and Raymond Wolfinger. 1992. *The Myth of the Independent Voter.* Berkeley and Los Angeles: University of California Press.

Kellstedt, Paul. 2003. *The Mass Media and the Dynamics of American Racial Attitudes.* New York: Cambridge University Press.

Kernell, Samuel, and Laurie Rice. 2008. "Preaching to the Choir: Cable Television and the Partisan Polarization of the President's Audience." Paper presented at the annual meeting of the Midwest Politcial Science Association, Chicago, IL.

Key, V. O. 1955. "A Theory of Critical Elections." *Journal of Politics* 17 (1): 3–18.

———. 1966. *The Responsible Electorate.* Cambridge, MA: Belknap Press of Harvard University Press.

Kimball, David. 2004. "A Decline in Ticket Splitting and the Increasing Salience of Party Labels." In *Models of Voting in Presidential Elections: The 2000 U.S. Elections,* edited by Herbert Weisberg and Clyde Wilcox. Stanford, CA: Stanford University Press.

Kiousis, Spiro. 2004. "Explicating Media Salience: A Factor Analysis of *New York Times* Issue Coverage during the 2000 Presidential Election." *Journal of Communication* 54 (1): 71–87.

Krosnick, Jon. 1990. "Government Policy and Citizen Passion: A Study of Issue Publics in Contemporary America." *Political Behavior* 12 (1): 59–92.

Krosnick, Jon, and Matthew Berent. 1993. "Comparisons of Party Identification and Policy Preferences: The Impact of Survey Question Format." *American Journal of Political Science* 37 (3): 941–964.

Krosnick, Jon, and Lin-Chiat Chang. 2001. "A Comparison of the Random Digit Dialing Telephone Survey Methodology with Internet Survey Methodology as Implemented by Knowledge Networks and Harris Interactive." Paper presented at the annual meeting of the American Association for Public Opinion Research, Montreal, QC, Canada.

Krosnick, Jon, and Arthur Lupia. 2005. "The American National Election Studies (ANES) 1948–2004 Cumulative Data File [dataset]." Stanford University

and the University of Michigan. Available online at http://www.electionstudies
.org.

Krosnick, Jon, and Richard Petty, eds. 1995. *Attitude Strength: Antecedents and Consequences.* Hillsdale, NJ: Erlbaum.

Kruse, Kevin. 2005. *White Flight: Atlanta and the Making of Modern Conservatism.* Princeton, NJ: Princeton University Press.

Lacayo, Richard. 2001. "How Bush Got There." *Time*, 20 August.

Lassiter, Matthew. 2006. *The Silent Majority: Suburban Politics in the Sunbelt South.* Princeton, NJ: Princeton University Press.

Lau, Richard, David Andersen, and David Redlawsk. 2008. "An Exploration of Correct Voting in Recent U.S. Presidential Elections." *American Journal of Political Science* 52 (2): 395–411.

Lau, Richard, and David Redlawsk. 1997. "Voting Correctly." *American Political Science Review* 91 (3): 585–598.

Layman, Geoffrey. 2001. *The Great Divide*. New York: Columbia University Press.

Layman, Geoffrey, and Thomas Carsey. 2002a. "Party Polarization and 'Conflict Extension' in the American Electorate." *American Journal of Political Science* 46 (4): 786–802.

———. 2002b. "Party Polarization and Party Structuring of Policy Attitudes: A Comparison of Three NES Panel Studies." *Political Behavior* 24 (3): 199–236.

Layman, Geoffrey, Thomas Carsey, and Juliana Menasce Horowitz. 2006. "Party Polarization in American Politics: Characteristics, Causes and Consequences." *Annual Review of Political Science* 9 (1): 83–110.

Lee, Taeku. 2002. *Mobilizing Public Opinion: Black Insurgency and Racial Attitudes in the Civil Rights Era.* Chicago: University of Chicago Press.

Levendusky, Matthew. 2008. "Clearer Cues, More Consistent Voters: The Effects of Elite Polarization on Attitude Consistency in the Mass Public." Manuscript. University of Pennsylvania.

———. Forthcoming. "The Micro-foundations of Polarization." *Political Analysis*.

Lin, Ann Chih. 1998. "The Troubled Success of Crime Policy." In *The Social Divide: Political Parties and the Future of Activist Government*, edited by Margaret Weir. Washington, DC: Brookings Institution Press.

Luskin, Robert, and John Bullock. 2006. "Measuring Political Knowledge." Manuscript. University of Texas at Austin.

Marcus, George. 2000. "Emotions in Politics." *Annual Review of Political Science* 3 (1): 221–250.

Markus, Gregory, and Philip Converse. 1979. "A Dynamic Simultaneous Equation Model of Electoral Choice." *American Political Science Review* 73 (4): 1055–1070.

Masket, Seth. 2007. "It Takes an Outsider: Extralegislative Organization and Partisanship in the California Assembly." *American Journal of Political Science* 51:482–497.

Mayer, William. 2007. "The Swing Voter in American Presidential Elections." *American Politics Research* 35 (3): 358–388.

————. 2008. *The Swing Voter in American Politics*. Washington, DC: Brookings Institution Press.

McCarty, Nolan, Keith Poole, and Howard Rosenthal. 2006. *Polarized America: The Dance of Ideology and Unequal Riches*. Cambridge, MA: MIT Press.

McClosky, Herbert, Paul J. Hoffmann, and Rosemary O'Hara. 1960. "Issue Conflict and Consensus among Party Leaders and Followers." *American Political Science Review* 54 (2): 406–427.

McKelvey, Richard. 1986. "Covering, Dominance, and Institution-Free Properties of Social Choice." *American Journal of Political Science* 30 (2): 283–314.

Milbank, Dana, and Howard Kurtz. 2004. "Kerry Calls Stem Cell Policy Unscientific and Political." *Washington Post*, 5 October, A6.

Miller, Gary, and Norman Schofield. 2003. "Activists and Partisan Realignments in the United States." *American Political Science Review* 97 (2): 245–260.

Miller, Warren. 2000. "Temporal Order and Causal Inference." *Political Analysis* 8 (2): 119–140.

Miller, Warren, and J. Merrill Shanks. 1996. *The New American Voter*. Cambridge, MA: Harvard University Press.

Miroff, Bruce. 2007. *The Liberals' Moment: The McGovern Insurgency and the Identity Crisis of the Democratic Party*. Lawrence: University Press of Kansas.

Moon, Woojin. 2004. "Party Activists, Campaign Resources and Candidate Position-Taking: Theory, Tests and Applications." *British Journal of Political Science* 34 (4): 611–633.

Morton, Rebecca. 2006. *Analyzing Elections*. New York: W. W. Norton.

Muirhead, Russell. 2006. "A Defense of Party Spirit." *Perspectives on Politics* 4 (4): 713–727.

Mutz, Diana. 2005. "Social Trust and E-Commerce: Experimental Evidence for the Effects of Social Trust on Individuals' Economic Behavior." *Public Opinion Quarterly* 69 (3): 393–416.

————. 2006. "How the Mass Media Divide Us." In *Red and Blue Nation? Characteristics and Causes of America's Polarized Politics*, vol. 1, edited by Pietro Nivola and David Brady. Washington, DC: Brookings Institution Press; Stanford, CA: Hoover Institution.

————. 2007. "Effects of 'In-Your-Face' Television Discourse on Perceptions of a Legitimate Opposition." *American Political Science Review* 101 (4): 621–635.

Mutz, Diana, and Byron Reeves. 2005. "The New Videomalaise: Effects of Televised Incivility on Political Trust." *American Political Science Review* 99 (1): 1–15.

National Institutes of Health. 2005. "Stem Cell Basics." Available online at http://stemcells.nih.gov/info/basics/.

Nie, Norman, and Kristi Andersen. 1974. "Mass Belief Systems Revisited: Political Change and Attitude Structure." *Journal of Politics* 36 (3): 541–591.

Nie, Norman, Sidney Verba, and John Petrocik. 1979. *The Changing American Voter*. Cambridge, MA: Harvard University Press.

Niemi, Richard, and Anders Westholm. 1984. "Issues, Parties, and Attitude Stability: A Comparative Study of Sweden and the United States." *Electoral Studies* 3 (1): 65–83.

Nisbet, Matthew. 2004. "Public Opinion about Stem Cell Research and Human Cloning." *Public Opinion Quarterly* 68 (1): 131–154.

Page, Benjamin, and Calvin Jones. 1979. "Reciprocal Effects of Policy Preferences, Party Loyalties and the Vote." *American Political Science Review* 73 (4): 1071–1090.

Patterson, Thomas E. 1994. *Out of Order*. New York: Vintage Books.

Peress, Michael. 2006. "Securing the Base: Electoral Competition under Variable Turnout." Manuscript. Carnegie Mellon University.

Perlstein, Rick. 2001. *Before the Storm: Barry Goldwater and the Unmaking of the American Consensus* New York: Hill and Wang.

———. 2008. *Nixonland: The Rise of a President and the Fracturing of America*. New York: Scribner.

Petrocik, John. 1996. "Issue Ownership in Presidential Elections, with a 1980 Case Study." *American Journal of Political Science* 40 (3): 825–850.

Polsby, Nelson. 2003. *How Congress Evolves: Social Bases of Institutional Change*. New York: Oxford University Press.

Poole, Keith, and Howard Rosenthal. 1997. *Congress: A Political-Economic History of Roll Call Voting*. New York: Oxford University Press.

Pope, Jeremy, and Jonathan Woon. 2007. "Roll Calls and Party Reputations: Evidence from the 2006 Cooperative Congressional Election Study." Paper presented at the annual meeting of the American Political Science Association, Chicago, IL.

Popkin, Samuel. 1991. *The Reasoning Voter*. Chicago: University of Chicago Press.

Prior, Markus. 2007. *Post-Broadcast Democracy: How Media Choice Increases Inequality in Political Involvement and Polarizes Elections*. New York: Cambridge University Press.

Rae, Nicol. 1989. *The Decline and Fall of the Liberal Republicans: From 1952 to the Present*. New York: Oxford University Press.

———. 2007. "Be Careful What You Wish For: The Rise of Responsible Parties in American National Politics." *Annual Review of Political Science* 10 (1): 169–191.

Rahn, Wendy. 1993. "The Role of Partisan Stereotypes in Information Processing about Political Candidates." *American Journal of Political Science* 37 (2): 472–496.

Riker, William. 1986. *The Art of Political Manipulation*. New Haven, CT: Yale University Press.

Roberts, Jason, and Steven Smith. 2003. "Procedural Contexts, Party Strategy, and Conditional Party Voting in the U.S. House of Representatives, 1971–2000." *American Journal of Political Science* 47 (2): 305–317.

Rohde, David. 1991. *Parties and Leaders in the Postreform House*. Chicago: University of Chicago Press.

Rosenblum, Nancy. 2008. *On the Side of Angels: An Appreciation of Parties and Partisanship*. Princeton, NJ: Princeton University Press.

Rosensteil, Thomas. 2006. "How the Mass Media Divide Us—Two Alternative Perspectives." In *Red and Blue Nation? Characteristics and Causes of America's*

Polarized Politics, vol. 1, edited by Pietro Nivola and David Brady. Washington, DC: Brookings Institution Press; Stanford, CA: Hoover Institution.

Sanbonmatsu, Kira. 2002. *Democrats, Republicans and the Politics of Women's Place*. Ann Arbor: University of Michigan Press.

Schattschneider, E. E. 1960. *The Semi-sovereign People*. Fort Worth, TX: HBJ.

Schudson, Michael. 1998. *The Good Citizen: A History of American Civic Life*. New York: Free Press.

Sekhon, Jasjeet. 2005. "Making Inferences from 2 × 2 Tables: The Inadequacy of the Fisher Exact Test for Observational Data and a Principled Bayesian Alternative." Manuscript. Harvard University.

Shafer, Byron, and Richard Johnston. 2006. *The End of Southern Exceptionalism: Class, Race, and Partisan Change in the Postwar South*. Cambridge, MA: Harvard University Press.

Shapiro, Robert, and Yaeli Bloch-Elkon. 2006. "Political Polarization and the Rational Public." Paper presented at the annual meeting of the American Association for Public Opinion Research, Montreal, QC, Canada.

Siegelman, Lee, and Emmett Buell. 2004. "Avoidance or Engagement? Issue Convergence in U.S. Presidential Campaigns, 1960–2000." *American Journal of Political Science* 48 (4): 650–661.

Sinclair, Barbara. 1995. *Legislators, Leaders and Lawmaking: The U.S. House of Representatives in the Postreform Era*. Baltimore, MD: Johns Hopkins University Press.

———. 2006. *Party Wars: Polarization and the Politics of National Policy Making*. Norman: University of Oklahoma Press.

———. 2008. "Spoiling the Sausages? How a Polarized Congress Deliberates and Legislates." In *Red and Blue Nation? Consequences and Corrections of America's Polarized Politics*, vol. 2, edited by Pietro Nivola and David Brady. Washington, DC: Brookings Institution Press; Stanford, CA: Hoover Institution.

Slevin, Peter. 2006. "Moderates in Kansas Decide They're Not in GOP Anymore." *Washington Post*, October 19, A01.

Smith, Mark. 2007. *The Right Talk: How Conservatives Transformed the Great Society into the Economic Society*. Princeton, NJ: Princeton University Press.

Sniderman, Paul. 2000. "Taking Sides: A Fixed Choice Theory of Political Reasoning." In *Elements of Reason: Cognition, Choice and the Bounds of Rationality*, edited by Mathew McCubbins, Arthur Lupia, and Samuel Popkin. New York: Cambridge University Press.

Sniderman, Paul, Richard Brody, and Philip Tetlock. 1991. *Reasoning and Choice: Explorations in Political Psychology*. New York: Cambridge University Press.

Sniderman, Paul, and John Bullock. 2004. "A Consistency Theory of Public Opinion and Political Choice: The Hypothesis of Menu Dependence." In *Studies in Public Opinion*, edited by Willem E. Saris and Paul M. Sniderman. Princeton, NJ: Princeton University Press.

Sniderman, Paul, and Edward Carmines. 1997. *Reaching beyond Race*. Cambridge, MA: Harvard University Press.

Sniderman, Paul, and Matthew Levendusky. 2007. "An Institutional Theory of Political Choice." In *Oxford Handbook of Political Behavior*, edited by Russell Dalton and Hans-Dieter Klingemann. New York: Oxford University Press.

Snyder, James, and Michael Ting. 2002. "An Informational Rationale for Political Parties." *American Journal of Political Science* 46 (1): 90–110.

Soroka, Stuart. 2002. *Agenda-Setting Dynamics in Canada*. Vancouver, BC, Canada: UBC Press.

Stimson, James. 2004. *Tides of Consent*. New York: Cambridge University Press.

Stoker, Laura, and M. Kent Jennings. 2008. "Of Time and the Development of Partisan Polarization." *American Journal of Political Science* 52 (3): 619–635.

Stokes, Donald. 1963. "Spatial Models of Party Competition." *American Political Science Review* 57 (2): 368–377.

Stone, Walter, Ron Rapoport, and Alan Abramowitz. 1994. "The Reagan Revolution and Partisan Polarization in the 1980s." In *The Parties Respond: Changes in the American Party System*, edited by Sandy Maisel. Boulder, CO: Westview Press.

Stroud, Natalie Jomini. 2008. "Media Use and Political Predispositions: Revisiting the Concept of Selective Exposure." *Political Behavior* 30 (3): 341–366.

Sundquist, James. 1983. *Dynamics of the Party System*. Washington, DC: Brookings Institution Press.

Theriault, Sean. 2008. *Party Polarization in Congress*. New York: Cambridge University Press.

Tomz, Michael, and Paul Sniderman. 2005. "Brand Names and the Organization of Mass Belief Systems." Manuscript. Stanford University.

Toner, Robin. 2004. "Southern Democrats' Decline Is Eroding the Political Center." *New York Times*, 15 November.

———. 2007. "Democrats Seek the Middle on Social Issues." *New York Times*, 16 January.

USA Today. 2006. "Fate of Two Joes Reflects Drive for Partisan Purity." August 10, 8A.

Van Houweling, Robert, and Paul Sniderman. 2006. "The Political Logic of a Downsian Space." Manuscript. University of California, Berkeley.

Wagner, Michael. 2007. "The Conditional Echo Chamber: Partisan Issue Framing and Public Opinion." Paper presented at the annual meeting of the Midwest Political Science Association, Chicago, IL.

Wand, Jonathan. 2007. "The Allocation of Campaign Contributions by Interest Groups and the Rise of Elite Polarization." Manuscript. Stanford University.

Wattenberg, Martin. 1998. *The Decline of American Political Parties, 1952–1996*. Cambridge, MA: Harvard University Press.

Weisman, Jonathan. 2007. "Boehner Leads Effort to Polish GOP 'Brand.'" *Washington Post*, 1 June, A13.

Whirls, Daniel. 1986. "Reinterpreting the Gender Gap." *Public Opinion Quarterly* 50 (3): 316–330.

Wilgoren, Jodi, and Bill Keller. 2004. "Kerry and Religion: Pressure Builds for Public Discourse." *New York Times*, 7 October.

Wolfe, Alan. 1999. *One Nation, After All*. New York: Penguin Books.

Woolley, John. 2000. "Using Media-Based Data in Studies of Politics." *American Journal of Political Science* 44 (1): 156–173.

Woolley, John, and Gerhard Peters. 2005. "The American Presidency Project." Available online at http://www.presidency.ucsb.edu.

Woon, Jonathan, and Jeremy Pope. 2008. "Made in Congress? Testing the Electoral Implications of Party Ideological Brand Names." *Journal of Politics* 70 (3): 823–836.

Zaller, John. 1986. "Analysis of Information Items in the 1985 Pilot Study." Report to the National Election Studies Board of Overseers, University of Michigan.

———. 1992. *The Nature and Origins of Mass Opinion.* New York: Cambridge University Press.

Index